Eating in the Light of the Moon

Eating in the Light of the Moon

how women
can transform
their relationships
with food
through myths,
metaphors &
storytelling

ANITA JOHNSTON, Ph.D.

gürze books

Eating in the Light of the Moon
how women can transform their relationships with food through myths, metaphors & storytelling

Trade paperback edition published in 2000 by
Gürze Books
PO Box 2238
Carlsbad, CA 92018
(800) 756-7533
www.gurze.com

Cover design by Abacus Graphics, Oceanside, CA

Library of Congress
Cataloging-in-Publication Data

Johnston, Anita.
    Eating in the light of the moon : how women can transform their relationships with food through myths, metaphors & storytelling / Anita Johnston.
    p. cm.
    ISBN 0-936077-36-0
    1. Compulsive eating-alternative treatment. 2. Women-Mental health. 3. Storytelling-Therapeutic use. 4. Metaphor-Therapeutic use. 5. Weight loss. I. Title.
RC552.C65J64   1996
616.85'26-dc20   95-47846
                        CIP

The authors and publishers of this book intend for this publication to provide accurate information. It is sold with the understanding that it is meant to complement, not substitute for, professional medical and/or psychological services.

0 9 8 7 6 5 4

To my mother,
  Emilie Anita Green Johnston
  And my daughters,
  Liana Anita Orenstein
  Ariel Emilie Orenstein

*D*aylight is one thing,
moonlight another.
Things take on a different look
beneath the moon than beneath
the sun. And it well might be
that to the Spirit the light of
the moon would appear to yield
the truer illumination.
—*Thomas Mann*

Contents

Acknowledgments

$\mathcal{I}$ would like to acknowledge those who assisted me in the growth of this project: Mary Moccia and Nada Mangialetti, with whom I cofounded the Anorexia and Bulimia Center of Hawaii, for their help in providing fertile ground for sowing the seeds for this book; Gail Cannon, for sharing my vision during germination and giving shelter to fragile seedlings; Dale Gilmartin, for providing poetic inspiration and encouragement so the roots could take hold; Sharon Dougherty, my transcriptionist, for helping to create a structure strong enough to support expansion; Marian Miller, for sharing personal and professional insights that provided the nourishment for vigorous growth; Dick Rapson, a seasoned gardener, for introducing me to Faith Hamlin, my former agent, who could envision blooms before by buds appeared; and Jim Ellison, for editing out the weeds with a keen eye and an open heart.

I would like to thank Norma Jean Stodden, Patty Kincaid, Velvalee, Marilyn and Morty Orenstein, Mare Grace and the women in my New Moon group, who all visited my garden from time to time and provided me with much appreciated encouragement and support. And I would like to express my gratitude to Roger Jellinek, my agent, and Lindsey Hall and Leigh Cohn at Gürze Books for showing me the rainbow after the storm.

Most of all, I would like to thank my husband, colleague, friend, and lover, Steve Orenstein, who was with me every step of the way to help cultivate my vision, pull out the weeds of doubt, provide an endless supply of editorial and technical support, and give the warmth, light, and love all things need to grow.

And last, I would like to express my heartfelt thanks to all the women who over the years trusted me with their stories and helped me to understand what it takes to truly nourish oneself and come into full bloom, especially those who have given me permission to use disguised versions of their stories in this book.

Preface

$\mathcal{M}$y interest in disordered eating evolved out of my clinical work with women's issues in therapy, those issues related to the experience of being female in our society today. Disordered eating emerged as a struggle prevalent among women. As more and more girls and women with eating disorders came to see me, I found myself fascinated by them because, contrary to what I had been led to believe by my colleagues and what much of the literature had indicated, they were not terribly difficult, resistant clients but some of the brightest, most talented, most creative people I had ever met. This, however, was not how they perceived themselves. They saw themselves as incompetent, worthless, and unattractive. Intrigued by this discrepancy between my perception and theirs, I listened carefully to their stories.

By offering up their life stories for scrutiny, these women were hoping to find some clues, some answers, to the origin of this mysterious obsession that consumed their lives. One woman would tell of the abuse she suffered from her father, while another would describe a father who encouraged her and applauded her every accomplishment. One woman would describe an alcoholic mother who was preoccupied with survival and had little nurturing to give her while another would tell of her experience with a doting, sometimes overprotective mother. There were women who suffered the loss of a parent through death or divorce and women whose families remained close-knit units. For every tale of woe there was a tale of a life with few apparent hardships.

While no particular pattern emerged from the details of their stories, I began to notice an underlying theme, a certain flavor to their diverse experiences that remained constant. The common thread seemed to be a pervasive sense of not quite fitting in, of not quite seeing things the way others did, of being a "misfit."

I learned that as very young girls, these women were bright and gifted and had an exceptional ability to perceive subtle realities. More often than not, a woman who struggled with disordered eating was once a girl who saw the invisible, who read between the lines, who sensed when things were not right. She noticed when people said one thing but did another. She could discern certain patterns of behavior and anticipate what was to come next. She knew when someone was being insincere or dishonest.

Her family, for one reason or another, did not appreciate her gift. They did not want to be confronted with discrepancies in their behavior or to address what seemed to be odd concerns or avant-garde ideas. They did not want to deal with her ultrasensitivity to emotional undercurrents, and at times they were threatened by her precociousness. Whenever she spoke the truth or questioned what was going on, she received a very clear message (often nonverbal) that this outspoken and questioning behavior was not okay and even dangerous to the stability of the family.

Since this child's survival depended on fitting into the family, she had to find a way to dim her light so her parents wouldn't be overwhelmed, so her brothers and sisters wouldn't feel jealous and reject her, so serious problems in the functioning of the family wouldn't be revealed and result in its possible disintegration. She collaborated with the other family members by taking a position that something was wrong with *her* perception, that something was wrong with *her*. After all, no one else in the family saw things the way she did.

As she searched for something to distract her from her discomfort and to diminish her perceptions, the girl began to feel the first stirrings of her obsession with food.

She may have been a young girl who intuited from her mother's behavior that her parents' marriage was a loveless one. This frightened her so much that she ate compulsively in an attempt to stuff down the truth that threatened to tear her family apart. Even though she suffered greatly from school yard taunts about her weight, at least she was able to keep this secret from entering her awareness on a daily basis and from being revealed to other family members.

She may have been a girl who discerned that in order to please her ambitious, workaholic stepfather, she needed to squelch her natural artistic tendencies. She discovered that keeping herself in a constant state of hunger could distract her from any need for creative expression that might cause conflict between them and interfere with her achievement of the goals he valued. Although her anorexia eventually created much concern and distress in her family, at least she was able to maintain her much coveted connection with him by hiding this "differentness" from herself as well as from him.

She may have been a girl gifted with beauty, intelligence, and lots of friends who noticed that her single mother withdrew affection whenever she became excited about her social activities and that her older sister acted resentful whenever she was successful academically. She discovered that having a "problem" with food kept their feelings of jealousy at bay because they would no longer be threatened by her "perfection." Having something with which to struggle enabled her to join their "ain't life tough" club and reduced the chances of their rejecting her.

For each of these girls, an obsession with food and fat created a new focus in her life. She could count calories and agonize over every pound rather than feel her deeper pain and fears. As she intensified her struggle with her body, her fear of being different and seeing things that others did not, and the feelings of loneliness that come with not quite fitting in, receded into the background.

Problems with food and fat, as painful as they could be, appeared to have a simple solution compared to the other problems in her life. All she had to do was stick to a diet and everything would be okay. Messages from the media in a culture obsessed with thinness supported this belief system.

As she became more deeply embroiled in this struggle with food, fat, and dieting, however, this "simple solution" became more and more elusive. She knew what she needed to do (lose more weight), but couldn't figure out how. And so she developed an image of herself as flawed, incompetent, and helpless. Once again, the society she lived in supported her contention that she was, indeed, inadequate because she lacked the willpower she needed to control her body.

The gift of her vision became buried beneath layers of self-doubt and self-loathing.

Upon becoming a woman, she found herself with a capacity to sense when things weren't quite right, to pick up on subtleties in conversations or tensions in relationships, to notice patterns in behavior or inconsistencies between what others said and did, but her *interpretations* of what she perceived became distorted by her self-doubt and low self-esteem. If she detected hostility beneath a friend's "helpful" criticism, she decided that she was being too sensitive. If her husband seemed troubled and withdrawn, she figured he was upset with her and no longer found her attractive. If she became angry at her mother's attempts to manipulate her, she assumed that she was overreacting.

And she would quell her emotional distress with thoughts of food.

With her eating behavior out of control and her self-esteem shattered, she found her way to the Anorexia and Bulimia Center of Hawaii, which I had cofounded with two other women. Upon entering therapy, she entered the labyrinth of recovery.

A labyrinth is an ancient and mysterious archetype. It consists of one pathway that loops back repeatedly upon itself, reaches the center and then winds its way back out again. Unlike a maze, there are no barriers, false turns, or dead ends. In many ancient religious traditions, the labyrinth was a powerful symbol of the journey of life, death, and rebirth. It was used as a meditation tool whose path would lead to one's own center and then back out into the world.

The women on the road to recovery from disordered eating began with a journey that required them to follow a twisting, turning, winding path to their centers. It required them to leave behind old perceptions of themselves that they had adopted from others and to reclaim their own inner authorities. They had to listen to the voice from within to give them guidance and support as they searched for their true thoughts, feelings, and desires. They found themselves letting go of all expectation of linear progress, disengaging the rational mind, and embracing the power of their emotions and intuition.

By listening to myths, fairy tales, and old folktales, they learned the language of metaphor, a language they needed in order to understand and absorb their inner truths, to find their own mythic reality, and to understand the deep wisdom of their personal stories.

As they walked this labyrinth, there were times they felt trapped, lost, bored, disoriented, frustrated, or anxious, but they kept on going, placing one foot in front of the other. Finding their centers, the essence of who they are as women, was not the end of the journey. They then had to exit the labyrinth, integrating this new vision with a new way of being in the world.

This book is for all those who dared to view their disordered eating in a different light so that they could reclaim their visions and their power. It includes some of the old myths, folk stories, and fairy tales I use in my work, stories that have been used through the ages to help women find their inner truth.

This book is for all those women who have dared to open to their full potential, to listen to the wise woman inside of them, to speak their truth, and to help heal this earth—and for those who want to.

Eating in the Light of the Moon

1

Woman Spirit

The Root of the Hunger

Today, more women than ever find themselves in a struggle with their weight. Diet books and programs for weight loss are a multi-billion-dollar industry. Anorexia, bulimia, and compulsive eating have reached epidemic proportions. In America, millions of women struggle with anorexia and bulimia, and thousands of them die from complications resulting from these disorders. Statistics indicate that 95 percent of those who have been diagnosed with eating disorders are female.

Obsession with the body, continual dieting, and excessive exercise routines have become so widespread among women that they are now considered normal behavior. Bodies sculpted by plastic surgery to look like those of prepubescent boys with breasts have become the standard for the ideal female body. Since the average model or actress is thinner than 95 percent of the population, most women know the frustration of living in a body that refuses to conform to the ideal.

It is impossible to discuss the causes for disordered eating without questioning the experience of being female in our society today. What is going on? Studies show that American women value being thin over being successful or loved and that most girls are unhappy with their bodies by age thirteen. Why are so many females so dissatisfied with their bodies? Is it because there is such an emphasis on thin, angular bodies, which very few women come by naturally?

If so, why has a naturally masculine shape (broad shoulders, no waist, narrow hips, flat belly) become the ideal for the female body? Why is it that those aspects of a woman's body that are most closely related to her innate female power, the capacity of her belly, hips, and thighs to carry and sustain life, are diminished in our society's version of a beautiful woman?

The answers can be found by taking a look at history from a perspective much broader than what we were taught as children. The history we were taught in school belongs to the patriarchy. It is a history that concerns itself with the struggle for power and domination. Our history books are filled with winners and losers of the great wars and the names of the men who fought in them.

The history of the patriarchy is limited to the last five thousand years. New archaeological data and research are revealing a much broader scope. Rather than reviewing civilization in terms of centuries, researchers Merlin Stone, Marija Gimbutas, Riane Eisler, and others are looking at the process of civilization over many millennia, as far back as thirty thousand years, before the advent of Judaism, Christianity, and the classical age of Greece.

A long time ago, these researchers tell us, the experience of women on this earth for thousands and thousands of years was very different than it is today. In their world, that which was female, and all its manifestations, was honored and revered. The female side of God, in the form of the Goddess, was worshipped. The spirit of the feminine was recognized as the creative life force of the earth.

Its symbol was the circle, a shape that has no beginning and no end. That which was round or curved was considered beautiful: the shape of the earth, an egg, the naturally rounded, curved shape of a woman's body. That which moved in cycles was respected and honored as a source of wisdom. The seasons, the moon phases, the ebb and flow of the tides, and nature's life-death-rebirth cycle were looked to for the answers to the mysteries of life.

Women's wisdom, gained from their natural connection to nature through their menstrual cycle, was revered. Women were respected for the power of their intuition and their understanding of the earth's ways. This wisdom was passed on from woman to woman, from mother to daughter, for thousands of years.

Time passed and things changed.

A new way of perceiving the world came into being. The line came to be considered superior to the circle. A hierarchy developed. What was made by men was considered superior to what was made by nature.

The circle was removed from a position of reverence and replaced by the symbol of the line, which had a beginning and an end, a top and a bottom, a superior position and an inferior position. And all things came to be valued according to their position. Those on top had more power than those on the bottom.

The Goddess was banished. Only the male side of God was allowed to be worshipped. The Earth was no longer viewed as the sacred source of all creation. It became an object to be divided up into many square pieces for those men with the most power to own and use. Women's connection to the wisdom of the earth through her body and the cycles of nature was rejected. The power of her intuition and emotions was ridiculed.

Women who taught the way of the circle, who used their connection to the earth for healing, who celebrated the feminine spirit, were imprisoned or killed. Generation after generation after generation watched their mothers and sisters burn at the stake for celebrating and embracing their feminine power.

More time passed and little changed.

Women still live in a society where what is masculine, linear, rational, and logical is considered superior to what is feminine, circular, intuitive, and emotional. Today's woman is a round peg trying desperately to fit into a square hole in order to survive and flourish.

How does she do this? By trying to shape her body into a more angular, masculine form, one that has zero fat to round off its edges. By being shamed into pretending that her menstrual blood (which once kept her so connected to the earth's ways) doesn't exist. By denying her most powerful emotions and quieting her intuitive voice.

Because she has banished her feminine spirit, she lives in a state of perpetual spiritual hunger. Her starving soul yearns for nourishment. But the nourishment of the Goddess, of the Woman Spirit, is not available to her. All there is is the food she feeds her body.

Is it any wonder that she overcompensates for her starvation? Is it any wonder that in frustration she goes on strike and decides to stop eating? Is it any wonder that her body becomes a battleground for the war between food and fat?

2

The Buried Moon

Rediscovering the Feminine

This folktale is called "The Buried Moon." It is about the nature of the feminine as represented by the moon. The light of the moon is soft and subtle. It gently illuminates that which is hidden, and it guides us through the dark corners of our unconscious.

Long, long ago, there was a wonderful land where people loved each other, and all things in nature were honored and respected. This land was, however, surrounded by bogs and swamps, and the people feared the great pools of black bog water and squishy tufts of marsh moss that squirted out creeping trickles of green water when they stepped on them.

In this land, the moon shone just as she does now, and the people depended on the light of the moon to walk about safely among the bog pools and marshes. But when she didn't shine, out came vile, evil creatures that dwelled in the darkness and went about seeking harm.

When the moon heard of the treachery and terror that filled the land in her absence, she felt great sorrow and decided to see for herself if it was truly as bad as people said it was. So when the dark of the month came, she wrapped herself in a black hooded cloak, taking care to tuck in her yellow, shining hair, and went straight to the bog edge.

There, it was dark—all dark but for the glimmer of the stars in the pools and the light that came from her own white feet, stealing out from under her black cloak. She trembled as she made her way, stepping lightly from tuft to tuft between the greedy, gurgling water holes. Just as she came near a big black pool, her foot slipped and she would have tumbled in had she not grabbed a nearby snag to steady herself. But as soon as she touched the snag, it twined itself around her wrists and arms, holding her fast. The more she pulled and twisted, the tighter it held.

As she pondered her fate, from far off in the distance she heard a faint, sobbing voice calling for help. She then heard footsteps and through the darkness saw a face with eyes wide with terror. It was a man who had strayed into the bogs. Dazed with fear, he struggled toward the flickering light that seemed to promise help and safety, unaware that he was straying farther from the path and into the black pool.

Frantic to warn him, the moon struggled even harder. Though she could not free herself, she twisted in such a way that her hood fell back off her yellow, shining hair, and the beautiful light that came from it drove away the darkness. The poor traveler was so relieved to see the vile creatures retreat into the darkness and to find his path out of the marsh, that he hurried on home as fast as he could.

Although the moon was happy that the lost soul had found his way, she, too, wanted to be free of the bogs, and so she began to fight and pull harder than ever. At last, she collapsed in exhaustion, and as she fell forward, her black hood fell over her head.

So out went the blessed light and back came the darkness and all its evil creatures. They attacked the moon with rage and spite and drove her deep down into the mud. When the sky began to show a pale gray light, the evil ones placed a large boulder on top of her and scurried away.

Days and days passed and the new moon never came. Without the moon's light, nighttime was no longer safe. Under cover of darkness, travelers got lost, things were stolen, and vile, evil creatures terrorized the land. Many people suffered. Everyone became frightened of the darkness that seemed to swallow up the land at night.

The people of the land sought help from the wise woman who lived in the old mill, and she instructed them on how to find the lost moon. They trekked into the marshes, armed with stones and hazel twigs, feeling fearful and creepy, until, at last, they came to the pool beside the snag where the moon lay buried. Catching a glimpse of a thin lip of light around the boulder, they took hold of the big stone and shoved it up.

For one short moment, they saw a strange and beautiful face looking up at them with gladness out of the black water and heard the angry wail of the fleeing evil horrors. And then they saw the moon rise into the sky, bright and beautiful as ever, making the bogs and pathways safe once again.

Since ancient times, the moon has been a symbol of the feminine. It is cyclical and ever changing with a strong sense of mystery. Its light is cool, reflective, and diffuse as contrasted with the bright, bold, and intensely focused light of the sun, which has often been associated with the masculine principle.

In our culture, we value sunshine, daylight, and summertime over moonlight, nighttime, and winter. We notice if the sun is up or down, whether it will be a sunny or overcast day, but pay little attention to the moon and its phases. Likewise, we have come to value only the masculine principles of direct action; single-minded focus; clear, logical thinking; goal-oriented, competitive behavior; linear structure; productivity; and achievement. We are uncomfortable with the feminine qualities of stillness, ambiguity, and emotion. We become impatient with cooperative, relationship-oriented attitudes, and see aesthetics, intuition, nurturance, and earthiness as unimportant.

Many traditional cultures recognize the necessity of both masculine and feminine aspects in all life. The tale of the buried moon reminds us that there was once a time when moonlight was considered essential, when the qualities of the feminine were appreciated and valued; a time when feeling was as important as thinking, intuition was as well regarded as logic, "being" was as much valued as "doing," and the journey was as significant as the destination.

According to Eastern philosophies, everything in the universe is based on the polarities of yin (feminine/receptive) and yang (masculine/active) energies. Yin is that which is open, yielding, connected. It embodies the intuitive, feeling, deep wisdom that comes from within. This is the feminine power that is connected to the subtle and seemingly invisible forces and rhythms of nature. It is concerned with harmony in all relationships. Yin can be symbolized by circles, spirals, or labyrinths that have no beginning and no end.

Yang is active, independent, and direct. It is the logical, intellectual energy that seeks out information and strives for control. Its power comes from doing and fixing. It is associated with separation, identity, autonomy, and individuality. It can be symbolized by the arrow with its linear angles thrusting upward and outward.

The tale of the buried moon warns of the danger to society when the balance between the masculine and feminine is not honored, if the feminine becomes buried, and the qualities of the masculine are considered more important than the qualities of the feminine. Great technological advances may be made, but if the feminine emphasis on feelings, relationships, and harmony is ignored, much violence and suffering can follow.

This story, like many legends and tales, is more than a story with a message for the community. It speaks to our own individual psyches and warns of the dangers of neglecting the feminine within ourselves. We all, men and women, carry both the masculine and feminine principles within us and are continually challenged to develop both aspects so that they can work in harmony. Neither quality is right or wrong. Neither quality is better or more valuable than the other. Problems develop when there is an imbalance between the two, when one aspect is valued more than the other, or when one side is dominated by the other.

The feminine spirit within us promotes nurturing, supportive relationships. The masculine promotes autonomy, separation, and individuality. If we develop our feminine side and not our masculine side we may find ourselves caught up in relationships where we focus on taking care of others without setting limits and find that we lose our sense of self. If we develop only the masculine, we find ourselves caught up in competitive power struggles and feel a pervasive sense of alienation that comes from not connecting with others in a heartfelt way. Our lives become little more than a rat race. An individual who is able to perceive the bigger picture and be receptive to his or her inner guidance but cannot take action can experience as many difficulties as someone who is all action and impulse with no inner sense of direction or meaning in his or her life.

The feminine within us is that wise, intuitive voice that perceives the truth. It is the open, receptive side that receives information from within and from without and holds it in a deep, knowing way. Her task is to be a vessel that contains our truth, our vision, our essence.

The masculine within us is the part of ourselves that takes action. It is very willful, focused, and directed. It is the intellectual, rational side that explains and organizes our thoughts and feelings logically. The task of the masculine is to be a vehicle that can boldly carry our truth out into the world in a clear, straight-forward way.

When there is balance and these two sides act in concert, we have what is called the "divine marriage," where the masculine honors and supports the feminine, providing protection for the journey out into the world. In an ideal situation:

- The feminine says, "I am lonely." The masculine side sits down and writes a letter to a friend.
- The feminine produces a dream. The masculine translates and organizes it.
- The feminine feels upset when a friend does something that hurts her feelings. The masculine puts those feelings into words and explains why that behavior was hurtful.
- The feminine says, "I am hungry." The masculine responds by getting and preparing the food or by asking, "Is this physical or emotional hunger?"

We live in a society where the balance between the feminine and the masculine has not been maintained. Masculine principles have been overly encouraged and feminine principles have been suppressed. Much emphasis is placed on goal-oriented activities, accomplishments, and productivity. Doing is more important than being. What we accomplish matters more than our manner or intent. Matters of the mind take precedence over matters of the heart. Success in money matters is respected more than success in relationships. Technological advancement is valued more than inner wisdom. Our civilization has "lost its moon." We are on the brink of disaster because the active, aggressive, outwardly thrusting energy has not been kept in balance with the inner, deep nurturing forces that sustain life and support harmonious relationships among all things.

This imbalance has been internalized within our psyches. As a result of living in such a culture, we have been encouraged to allow our masculine sides to dominate, control, and judge our feminine natures. Rather than experiencing and expressing our feelings, we are taught to reject and control them because they are irrational. Instead of honoring our dreams and intuitions, we ignore or ridicule them because they are not logical. Rather than trusting our bodies to inform us when we are in need of physical nourishment or stimulation, we follow elaborate diet plans and rigid exercise regimes. We look to facts and figures and disregard our gut reactions when attempting to validate our perceptions. Consequently . . .

- When your inner feminine says, "I'm lonely," the masculine insists that you have no reason to feel that way.
- When you have a thought-provoking dream, your masculine laughs at it or dismisses it as "only" a dream.
- When you are upset with a friend's behavior, you tell yourself that you are just too sensitive.
- When you feel hungry, you criticize yourself for eating too much.

The epidemic of disordered eating among women is clearly a consequence of the imbalance between the feminine and the masculine within our society and *within ourselves.* Many women are experiencing the despair and alienation that comes not only from the suppression of the feminine in the world we live in, but also from the rejection of their own inner feminine nature. By ignoring our feminine voice time and time again, we run the risk of losing it or finding it buried in the muck, just like the people in the story. When we stop listening to our feelings and intuitions, our psyches are plunged into a darkness that can be frightening. In this darkness, our feelings, hungers, and desires become mysterious, destructive forces, ready to wreak havoc upon our bodies and minds.

Women who struggle with disordered eating, more often than not have an overly dominant inner masculine aspect that continually attempts to control the inner feminine. Their masculine side is unrelentingly critical, even hostile, toward their feminine side. Consequently, their lives are filled with activities, chores, and endless lists of things they must get done. Moments of reverie, relaxation, or quiet time are either condemned as a "waste of time" or avoided because feelings or desires may surface that might question or in some way interfere with their ambitions or goals. Nighttime becomes particularly treacherous because, without the busyness of rushing here and there, doing this and that, dreaded urges to eat fill up the space that is not allowed to remain empty and still.

When the masculine controls the feminine, there is a lot of action without meaning. We find ourselves eating compulsively or counting calories obsessively, rather than tuning in to our bodies (so that we eat when we are hungry and stop when we are full) or listening to our inner guidance (to find out why we want to eat when we are not physically hungry). We play the outwardly focused numbers game of how many pounds, how many calories, to determine how well our day is going. We participate in an endless cycle of diets where we try to control rather than honor our inner desires and appetites. We try to sculpt our female bodies so that they are more linear and angular, less round and curvaceous. We believe that willful perseverance is the best approach to everything, that having a lot of "willpower" (as evidenced by weight loss) is the ultimate compliment. We attempt to control our feelings and instincts by restricting our food intake (it's pretty difficult to attend to other feelings when you're hungry). And when our inner feminine begins to rebel, we accuse her of being irrational, too sensitive, out of control, lacking in willpower.

Recovery from disordered eating calls for a deliberate, conscious attempt to reclaim our feminine side so we can bring our masculine side back into balance. Like the people in the story, we must consult our inner wise woman who can tell us how to bring back the moon.

3

The Beginning
Revisioning the Struggle

This Hans Christian Andersen fairy tale is about a very vain emperor who didn't care much about ruling his people well. Instead he was interested mostly in fine jewels and fancy clothing. One day two con men came into town who claimed they made the most exquisite clothing, clothing that was so fine only those who were fit for the office they held could see them. Stupid, ignorant people could not see the fine clothes.

The emperor was taken in by these two and commissioned them to make him a new wardrobe. The two con men pretended to weave the cloth on looms and stitch the fabric. All the courtiers who worked for the emperor raved about the beautiful patterns and colors for they didn't dare give any indication that they were not fit for their office. The emperor himself expressed great satisfaction (not wanting to reveal his stupidity) and dressed himself in his new clothes for the procession through town. As he paraded through the streets the townspeople oohed and aahed so their neighbors would not think they were ignorant folk. Except for one small child who turned to her mother and said in a loud voice, "But the emperor has nothing on at all!" This comment created a ripple throughout the crowd and eventually all the townspeople saw the truth as it was.

For a woman struggling with disordered eating, this story has much relevance. At some early point in her life (usually beginning around age four) she was like the small child in the village. She could see things as they really were and was not taken in by others' descriptions of reality. She would pick up on discrepancies between what people said and what they did. She could sense when something was wrong even when everyone around her said everything was okay.

But unlike the child in the story, when this young girl spoke the truth or brought to light that things were not as they seemed, her truth was not well received. Instead, her statements were either ignored or met with fear and hostility from family members or authority figures. She got the message (usually nonverbal) that her ability to perceive the truth, her particular sensitivity to that which was outside the awareness of others, was dangerous, that it could bring about ridicule and rejection, abuse, or even disintegration of the family (a very dangerous consequence from a four-year-old's perspective).

This put the young girl in a very uncomfortable position. In order to survive, she had to find a way to conceal who she really was, to diminish this ability to see the invisible, to quiet that voice inside of her that spoke the truth. She had to hide her sixth sense, her female intuition, not only from others but also from herself. For acknowledging her differentness (even secretly to herself) would have resulted in extreme emotional distress—a sense of not belonging or fitting in—that would have been unbearable. And so began the process of disowning the wise woman inside of her.

How did she do this? She did it by accepting others' perceptions of reality and rejecting her own. This was easy if her perceptions could not be validated by the five senses or logic and if others around her were insistent that theirs' was the only accurate perception of reality. She stopped listening to her inner voice for guidance and started to follow the rules of others. She denied herself her greatest heart's desires and replaced them with lengthy mental lists of "shoulds" and "shouldn'ts." She strived to become a totally rational human being without any regard for the emotional and spiritual aspects of her being. She viewed her appetite and desires as evil and thus perceived her body and its female manifestations as the enemy rather than as her physical connection to a greater source of knowing.

This rejection of a large part of her being, however, eventually takes its toll. As the years go by, she is plagued with a vague, uneasy sense of emptiness. So she tries to fill herself up. Since she is no longer clear about what she longs for she assumes her hunger is a physical one. And so she either eats compulsively or becomes horrified at her seemingly insatiable appetite and proceeds to starve herself.

She then continues through life with the assumption that there is something very wrong with her. After all, if she sees things a certain way and no one else does, there must be something wrong with her. Her struggle with food confirms that indeed, there is something wrong with her. This then becomes her focus, her obsession: if only she could fix this problem, then everything would be okay.

One of the first things a woman on the path of recovery from disordered eating must do is to reframe her concept of who she really is. She must recognize her bright, intuitive nature for the gift that it is even though others' discomfort with it has brought upon her some struggles and emotional wounding. She must begin to assert, both to herself and the world around her, that she is not defective. She must begin to review and retell the story of her life from the understanding that there is nothing wrong with her, that although she has been hurt, she is not damaged goods. Her disordered eating behavior is not evidence that she is a faulty human being in desperate need of repair.

The recovering woman needs to recognize that her obsession with food and fat does not define who she is. Her perspective must shift so that she can see this obsession not as some horrible character defect but, rather, as a simple, and much-needed protective mechanism she picked up along her journey through life. It is something she has learned to use to help her deal with the emotional distress of being different or feeling misunderstood, unaccepted, or overwhelmed. She needs to consider the possibility that the development of disordered eating patterns may not necessarily have been such a poor choice, given the limited options, resources, or coping skills she had available to her during stressful periods or times of crisis in her life.

Imagine yourself standing in the rain on the bank of a raging river. Suddenly, the water-swollen bank gives way. You fall in and find yourself being tossed around in the rapids. Your efforts to keep afloat are futile and you are drowning. By chance, along comes a huge log and you grab it and hold on tight. The log keeps your head above water and saves your life. Clinging to the log you are swept downstream and eventually come to a place where the water is calm. There, in the distance, you see the riverbank and attempt to swim to shore. You are unable to do so, however, because you are still clinging to the huge log with one arm as you stroke with the other. How ironic. The very thing that saved your life is now getting in the way of your getting where you want to go. There are people on shore who see you struggle and yell, "Let go of the log!" But you are unable to do so because you have no confidence in your ability to make it to shore.

This is not unlike the position many people find themselves in when they first become aware of their disordered eating. They feel foolish at best, humiliated at worst, that they are unable to stop a behavior that is interfering with their desire to get where they want to go in life. In the face of their shame, they quickly forget the role their disordered eating played in their survival, how it helped them keep their heads above water through some rough times by giving them a way to deal with their conflicts, feelings, and difficult situations. They immediately assume that there must be something wrong with them to continue such "destructive" behavior. This view, unfortunately, is supported by well-meaning friends, family, and professionals who suggest that they "just stop doing it": stop starving themselves, stop bingeing and purging, stop eating compulsively, stop gaining weight.

Simply letting go of the log may not, in fact, be the best course of action to take. What would happen if you let go of the log, began to swim to shore, and got halfway there only to find that you didn't have the strength to make it all the way? This means that you won't be able to make it back to the log, either. Many people feel foolish for clinging to the log, and many of their friends, family, and even health professionals become frustrated with their "resistance" to letting go. They assume the tenacity with which they cling to their disordered eating is a personality flaw, rather than a sign from within that more preparation is needed.

Recovery from disordered eating requires honoring rather than condemning the resistance encountered. It insists upon a recognition that any behavior that slows, stalls, or creates obstacles in the path toward recovery has meaning and a purpose that can be valuable, even essential.

A woman who seeks recovery needs to understand clearly the ways in which her disordered eating has served her so that she can stop viewing it as simply an impediment to her happiness. Only then can she know precisely which skills she needs to develop in order to live a life free from bingeing, dieting, and food obsessions.

One woman may discover that her fat has helped her avoid unwanted sexual advances from men. This tells her that assertiveness is a skill she needs to develop before she can let go of her weight "problem". Another woman may discover that she has binged and purged to eliminate inner tension she experiences when faced with conflict. This means that in order to resolve her bulimia, she needs to learn some conflict-resolution skills. Yet another woman may recognize that her obsession with dieting helped her cope with an intrusive, alcoholic mother, and for her, recovery entails learning how to set boundaries in relationships.

To recover from disordered eating requires the development of whatever skills are necessary to replace the function of the log. Once a woman develops these skills she will discover that they are much more effective and efficient than the disordered eating behavior, and will tend to choose to use *them* to help her cope with whatever stressors life throws her way. She can then let go of the log, relying on her newfound skills to keep her afloat and to give her the strength she needs to make it to shore.

And so, very slowly and carefully, you let go of the log and practice floating. When you start to sink, you grab back on. Then you let go of the log and practice treading water, and when you get tired, hold on once again. After awhile, you practice swimming around the log once, twice, ten times, twenty times, a hundred times, until you gain the strength and confidence you need to swim to shore. Only then do you completely let go of the log.

Recovery from disordered eating begins with the understanding that the disordered eating behavior served you when your goal was survival. This understanding is then followed by the development of new skills that will enable you not to simply survive, but to get what you want out of life, to thrive. Survival is no longer the only goal. The goal becomes one that includes a life that is rich and fulfilling.

It is a gradual, step-by-step process that calls for letting go of judgment ("there is something wrong with me"), the development of some important life skills, and learning to trust that inner voice that will tell you when you are ready.

4

The Red Herring

Food is Not the Issue

When we struggle with disordered eating it is often difficult to believe that food is not the issue that is causing us such grief. Certainly our struggle appears to be centered around what we are doing (eating compulsively, bingeing, and purging) or not doing (starving) with food. It seems as though, whether we are dieting or caught up in a binge, all we can think about is food.

Someone struggling with anorexia may deny her hunger and not eat, but she is secretly obsessed with food and fat. She spends much of her day counting calories, weighing herself, exercising excessively, preparing food for others, and thinking about the foods she didn't eat. Compulsive eaters find themselves thinking about the foods they are not supposed to be eating and scolding themselves for what they did eat and for how fat they look. Those who are caught up in the binge-purge process of bulimia spend enormous amounts of time planning and preparing for their binge and worrying about how they will be able to purge in secret. For concerned family members and friends who are witnessing this, all the evidence of an eating disorder points to food. And yet food is not the real issue. It is a smoke screen. It is the red herring.

A "red herring" describes something designed to confuse or divert attention from something else. Let's say you are following a whodunit and the question is "Who killed the old lady? Was it the maid, the butler, or the chauffeur?" As you are following the mystery along everyone is watching the maid because she was around the old lady the most and had been acting suspiciously. At the end of the story, there's a twist and it turns out not to have been the maid who committed the murder, but the butler, who no one suspected because they were busy scrutinizing the maid. The maid is the red herring. She's the distractor.

With disordered eating, food becomes the red herring. It can distract those struggling with an eating disorder as well as concerned family members and friends and even professionals who are trying to help. When we focus on what someone is doing with food we fail to see what the real culprit is. We become caught up in illusions that cause us to stray from the path of recovery, because we start looking for solutions in all the wrong places.

This old English fairy tale is about a girl who longed to touch the stars in the sky.

Every evening, just before falling asleep at night, she would lie in her bed and gaze out at the stars through her bedroom window. On clear nights she would be delighted to see them twinkling ever so brightly. Other nights she would watch them play hide-and-seek with the clouds. On stormy nights, they wouldn't show their faces at all even though she suspected they were still there, hiding behind the clouds.

One warm summer evening when the moon was full, the girl decided to satisfy her yearning and set out in search of the stars. She walked and walked until she came to a smooth, glassy pond. "Good evening," the girl said. "I'm off to find the stars in the sky. Can you tell me how to reach them?"

"They're right here in my face," replied the pond. "Jump in and catch them."

The girl looked at the stars glistening in the pond and jumped right in, her hands cupped so that she might catch one. But not a star did she find.

She went on her way until she came to a bubbling brook. "Good evening," said the girl. "I'm off to find the stars in the sky. Can you help me?"

"Oh, yes," answered the brook. They are always here, dancing in the water between the stones. Come on in and catch them."

So the girl waded into the brook, with her hands cupped so she could scoop them up. But not a star did she find.

"I don't think the stars are really here!" the girl cried in dismay.

"Well, they look like they are here, and that's just the same thing," said the brook.

"No, it's not," insisted the girl.

She continued on her way until she encountered a group of fairies dancing on a hill. "Good evening," said the girl as she approached the wee folk. "I'm off to find the stars in the sky. Can you help me?"

"They are right here, in the dew on the grass where we are dancing. Come and dance with us and you will catch one."

So the girl danced and danced with the ring of fairies, swooping down with her hands, trying to scoop up some stars. But not a star did she find. In frustration, she sat on a mossy stump and said to the fairies as they whirled by, "I've searched and searched for the stars but I cannot find them. Can't you help me?"

One of the fairies began to dance around her, and with a high, sweet voice said, "Since you are so determined to find the stars, I will tell you how to reach them: If you will not go backward, then go forward. Be sure to take the right road. Ask Four-Feet to carry you to

*No-Feet, who will carry you to the Stairs Without Steps. If you can
climb them, you will reach the stars."*

*The girl quickly stood up and began to go forward, making sure
she was on the right road. She came to a horse grazing underneath a
tree. "Good evening," she said. "I'm off to find the stars in the sky.
Can you carry me there?"*

*"I don't know the whereabouts of the stars in the sky," said the
horse. "My purpose is to serve the fairies."*

*"I was just dancing with them," said the girl, "and they told me
to ask Four-Feet to carry me to No-Feet."*

*"Well, I am Four-Feet, and if the fairies say I am to take you to
No-Feet, then climb on my back and off we'll go," said the horse.*

*The girl rode and rode until they came to the end of the land
where the sea stretched out in front of them as far as the horizon.
Way off in the distance was a ribbon of brilliant colors that arched
up into the sky.*

*The girl slid off the horse's back and stood at the water's edge. A
very large fish swam up to her. "Good evening," said the girl. "I'm
looking for the Stairs Without Steps. Can you take me there?"*

*"I am not available to serve anyone who asks. I am only to do
the bidding of the fairies," replied the fish.*

*"I was just dancing with them and was told to ride Four-Feet
who would carry me to No-Feet who would carry me to the Stairs
Without Steps."*

*"Well, in that case, hop on my back. I am No-Feet, and I will
carry you to the Stairs Without Steps," said the fish.*

*Off they went, the girl holding tightly to the fish's back until
they reached the horizon where the brilliant colors arched high up
into the sky. "Here they are," said the fish. "Be careful as you go up.
They are not easy to climb."*

The girl slid off the fish's back and began to climb the bright arch of many colors. The fish was right. They were not easy to climb. But she moved slowly and cautiously, inching her way along. As she became weary she would occasionally lose her grip and slip backwards. It was cold and she was surrounded by darkness, but she pressed on until she reached the top of the arch where she was surrounded by brilliant light. At last! There they were—the stars in the sky! She reached out with her hand to touch one of the shimmering stars. As she reached farther and farther, she suddenly lost her balance, and with a sigh that was half regret, half contentment, she fell, slipping and sliding, faster and faster into the darkness below.

When she opened her eyes, it was morning and she found herself in her bed. "I did reach the stars, didn't I?" she wondered. "Or did I only dream it?"

Then she looked at her hand that was still tightly clenched into a fist, and as she slowly opened it, she saw a speck of stardust.

Breaking free from struggles with food, fat, and dieting can seem as impossible as reaching for the stars. This story tells us that if you want to reach your dream you must not spend much time chasing an illusion. While the girl initially was fooled by the reflection of the stars on the pond, in the brook, and in the dew, she soon recognized that the reflection was not the same as the stars themselves. Problems with food are simply reflections of the real issues we struggle with. It is important to recognize that food is not the problem itself.

If I am obsessing about food, fat, and dieting, what I am doing with food is distracting me from the real issues I struggle with in my life. As horrible as feeling fat is, as painful as it is to struggle with feeling fat, focusing on feeling fat gives me something tangible, gives some definition to troubled feelings that may seem unresolvable. It seems to be a way, literally and figuratively, to "put my finger on" the source of the problem. But like stars in a pond, it is only an illusion.

Think of the "fat attack." Anyone who has struggled with disordered eating is familiar with fat attacks. A fat attack occurs when you all of a sudden feel extremely fat, as though you've just gained twenty pounds overnight. You know, rationally, that you did not actually gain twenty pounds overnight but it sure *feels* that way. Yesterday you might not have felt terrific, but you felt okay. Today, you feel horribly fat. What's going on?

When you are having a fat attack, this is a signal that something else is going on that is upsetting you. Maybe you are angry at something your mother said, maybe you are nervous about an upcoming date, maybe you are feeling frustrated with a supervisor at work, maybe you are feeling bad about something you said to a friend. If these are things you don't quite know how to handle comfortably, you may begin to focus intensely on your fat and the original problem will appear to fade into the background. As bad as it feels to see yourself as fat, at least you know what the solution is: lose weight.

A fat attack is different from generally feeling bad about your weight. It comes on rather suddenly and is very intense. It is not based on reality, even though the feelings that it generates are very real. It seems like the source of your misery, but like the starlight in dewdrops, it is only a reflection of something else that is troubling you.

What if the real problem is that you have a terrible relationship with your mother or you're in a marriage that's intolerable for you, or you hate your job, or you feel lonely even in a room full of people? These are much bigger, more complex issues that can often become overwhelming.

Here's where food comes into the picture. If you starve yourself, all you seem to think about is food. If you binge and purge, you spend much of your time planning your binges and finding the time and place to purge. If you are eating compulsively, you focus on food, food, food. And those other problems, at home, at school, at work, or in relationships, magically seem to disappear.

Coping with the "real problems" requires skills that you may not have, and resolving them may seem like an impossible task, as difficult as climbing a rainbow. When you embark on a journey to uncover and resolve underlying conflicts or feelings, and don't allow yourself to be fooled by any illusions of what is truly troubling you, you may learn something important about the function and purpose of your disordered eating. You may discover how it helps to distract you from the issues in your life that overwhelm you, that you haven't yet learned how to deal with effectively. And you may discover how effectively it distracts you, moment to moment, from the fear of facing things head on, from the pain of past hurts. No wonder it can be so addictive.

The relief you get, however, is only temporary. The disordered eating distracts you only temporarily from the emotional stress you are experiencing. It doesn't do anything to make the stress go away. Although what you are doing with food distracts you from your sadness, your anger, or your fear, it doesn't help to resolve problems. In fact, it helps to make them worse. The stress inside worsens and the disordered eating behavior increases. The real issues never do get resolved.

When we decide to follow our dream of being free from disordered eating, what is required is not just a longing to reach for the stars, but a willingness to go forward on the right path, to not get distracted by the illusion that thinness creates happiness, or be sidetracked by the beliefs that all we need is enough willpower to stick to a diet, that calorie counting is the answer, and that food is the problem.

5

Addiction

Spiritual and Emotional Hunger

Many women do not recognize the addictive nature of disordered eating until they find themselves in the throes of it, mercilessly driven by a compulsion for thinness and hounded by an appetite for food that seems insatiable. They find themselves unable to silence one inner tyrant that hollers, "I want more, more, more!" while trying to appease another who rejects anything short of the perfect body as not good enough.

Wanting desperately to be free from this addiction, they despise their voracious hunger and loathe their imperfect bodies. Because they misinterpret their hunger as physical, they see food as the enemy and their bodies as traitors in a war against fat. Caught up in the denial that is ever present in all addictions, they fail to recognize the starvation of their spirits. They cannot see the emptiness that is in their hearts. They make a fundamental error in failing to separate what is concrete from what is symbolic and become obsessed with the concrete object, the food itself. They do not see that the addictive object is a representation of something much greater, that it is only a *symbol* of what they truly desire. They do not understand that the terrible emptiness they feel is a spiritual or emotional emptiness, not a physical one.

The objects of addiction are sometimes interchangeable. Women will often go from one addiction to another. One may be in recovery from an addiction to alcohol or drugs and suddenly find herself immersed in an addiction to eating. Another may replace an addiction to eating with an addiction to exercise or may follow up a food binge with a shopping binge. So long as they do not identify the true hunger, the real longing, women cannot be free from the addictive process and may simply wind up substituting one addiction for another.

Addictions remove us from realities we find intolerable. They provide escape routes away from the conflicts and dilemmas we find unsolvable. When we cannot bear to be in our own skins, in our own bodies, where we experience both the pain and the wonder of being human, our addictions can throw us into a state of unconsciousness. When unconscious, we feel nothing, know nothing of our pains, confusion, struggles. Anyone who has experienced a binge knows the trance-like state it can induce where all other realities fade into the background, at least for as long as the binge lasts. Anyone who has starved herself knows the intoxicating "high" that becomes more and more difficult to resist. Those addicted to running are familiar with the sense of euphoria it can bring.

Women who are addicted to eating or dieting are terrified of their bodies. They withhold love from and try to abandon their bodies because it is in their bodies that their emotions reside. To be in contact with their bodies means to be in contact with their feelings, and this can be messy and painful. Emotions often can't be readily organized and understood, like thoughts. Unlike behaviors, they cannot be controlled.

All addictive processes represent an effort to keep feelings under control. Even more than that, they represent an effort to keep the flow of *life itself* under control. The addicted person is unable to let things be, unable to let things take their natural course. There is always some right way, some better way, some more perfect way that things can be.

Addictions keep us from being fully present in the moment with ourselves, our feelings, our friends, our lovers, or with whomever or whatever might have captured our attention. Instead, we find ourselves agonizing over how many calories we ate earlier in the day. Rather than being in contact with life, we withdraw from it, into our obsessive thoughts about bingeing and dieting. By putting our energies into planning that next binge or preparing for that next diet, we remove ourselves from the present, thrust our minds into the future and miss out on the life that could be unfolding before our eyes.

The paradox of all this is that only when we are in the here and now can we really get filled up and be nourished by life. Life takes place only in the present. If you are obsessing about yesterday or planning for tomorrow, you will be unable to take in and receive whatever is in front of you that can be nourishing: a smile from a child, a compliment from a friend, the scent of a rose, a favorite tune, a brilliant sunset. So the hunger continues. And the emptiness grows.

Even though we are talking about addictions, it is important to remember that, unlike such things as alcoholism and drug addiction, disordered eating is a *process* addiction. The woman with disordered eating is addicted to her eating behavior, and not to food itself.

With *substance* addictions, like alcoholism, removing the addictive substance (the alcohol) from the person's life is essential to recovery. Alcohol is what the alcoholic is addicted to; she is not addicted to drinking. Alcohol, unlike food, is not necessary for life. We can live without alcohol. We cannot live without food.

Some people try to treat eating disorders as if they are just like alcoholism and drug addiction. They make efforts to encourage things like "abstinence" and food plans. But this kind of approach often fails because too much emphasis gets placed on food itself and not on the addictive process, the disordered eating behavior. We find the same problem with dieting for weight loss. With restrictive diets, calorie counting, herbal supplements, and food plans, too much emphasis is placed on food, as if food were the problem.

Food is *not* the problem.

To recover from disordered eating, we must be willing to go beyond the food itself to discover the presence of the real hunger that underlies the urge to eat compulsively. With disordered eating behavior, our true needs and innermost desires are hidden behind urges that only symbolize those real needs and desires. When we are engaged in addictive eating, that is the time to look for what the real hunger is because that is the moment in which it gets presented to us in its symbolic form. By simply eliminating certain foods or striving to restrict our behavior, we deprive ourselves of opportunities to learn of the true meanings behind those symbols.

Someone who is addicted to eating is actually starving on an emotional and spiritual level. Her longing for food is a longing for emotional and spiritual nourishment. It is often a longing for the ideal mother, the archetypal Good Mother who nourishes us, soothes us, and loves and accepts us just the way we are. Frequently, this is the "something" she searches for as she stands in front of the fridge. This is what she is really in pursuit of when she sets out for the grocery store. No matter how much ice cream she eats, how many cookies she consumes or muffins she devours, she cannot fulfill this longing because she is filling her stomach, not her heart, not her spirit.

For a woman to recover from disordered eating, she must recognize that she is starving. She needs to understand that the food she requires is not material food. She must be able to name her hunger and recognize its symbolic nature in order to nourish herself.

This old Bantu folktale is about a great hunger a long, long time ago in Africa. A drought had left the land dry and fallow and no food could easily be found for the animals.

One day, all the animals, except the lion, decided to leave the jungle to scour the landscape in search of something to eat. The lion, who was king of the jungle, chose to remain behind and rule over his kingdom. And so, the elephant, the giraffe, the rabbit, the tortoise, the monkey, the zebra, and the gazelle set out together to scour the landscape for food to eat. They crossed the great river, and walked and walked across the flat land for many days, not knowing where their journey would take them.

After some time, as they approached the edge of the plain, the animals began to make out the figure of what appeared to be a tall tree, the only one that stood for miles around. And as their journey drew them closer to this tree they saw that it was laden with the most luscious fruit they had ever seen! Fruit as red as pomegranates, as orange as mangoes, as yellow as bananas, as purple as plums, and as fragrant as all the fruits of the world.

But, for all its beauty and promise, the tree left the animals crying in frustration and despair. For it was so tall and its branches so high off the ground that even the neck of the giant giraffe was not long enough to reach even the bottom-most fruit. And the trunk of the tree was so smooth that even the agile monkey could not climb it.

The famished animals collapsed on the ground beneath the tree. "What are we going to do?" they lamented. An old tortoise spoke: "My great-great-grandmother once told me about a tree such as this one, with beautiful and delicious fruit. But only those who knew the name of the tree could reach the fruit."

"How can we find the name of the tree?" the animals asked in unison.

The old tortoise answered, "The lion knows the name. Someone must travel back to the jungle to ask him."

It was decided that the gazelle, who was the fastest runner of all, should go. The gazelle, proud of his swiftness, raced to the jungle and to the place near the river that the lion king called home. "What do you want?" questioned the lion when the gazelle arrived.

"Great king," said the gazelle, "all the animals are so very hungry. We have been searching for days for something to eat. We have finally found the most beautiful tree, filled with wondrous, colorful fruit. But until we find the name of the tree, the fruit will remain out of our reach, and all the animals will continue to starve."

The lion thought quietly for a moment and then said, "I will tell you what you need to know. I do not wish to see the animals of my kingdom suffer any more. But I will only tell you once, for I do not wish to repeat myself or to tell anyone else this special name. You must listen carefully and remember. The name of the tree is Ungalli."

"Ungalli," said the gazelle. He thanked the lion and ran through the jungle and then back across the flat land thinking about how clever the other animals were to send an animal as swift as he and how happy and grateful they would be when he returned with the name of the tree. Lost in his thoughts, he did not see the rabbit hole that was near to where the animals lay waiting. He stepped in the hole and flipped head over hoof through the air until he landed with a thud at the foot of the tree.

The animals gathered around him. "What is the name of the tree?" they shouted with great hope and expectation.

But the gazelle just stared at the animals with a dazed look in his eyes. "What is the name of the tree?" the desperate animals shouted again and again.

"I can't remember," he uttered, in a voice barely above a whisper. "I can't remember."

The animals moaned. "We have no choice. We will just have to send someone else, someone who will remember no matter what," they said.

*It was decided that the elephant should go since it was well-
known that she did not forget anything. And so the elephant strode off
across the flat, empty plain, feeling quite proud of her excellent
memory. When the elephant arrived at the place near the river where
the lion king lived, the lion growled, "What do you want?"*

*"Oh, king," said the elephant, "the animals are all so hungry
and I . . ."*

*"I know, I know," said the lion impatiently. "I will tell you the
name of the tree with the wonderful fruit, but don't you forget because
I absolutely will not tell anyone else. The name of the tree is Ungalli."*

*"I will not forget," said the elephant with arrogance, "I never
forget anything." She made her way out of the jungle and across the
plain thinking to herself, "How could I forget! I can remember the
names of all the trees in this jungle." And she began to name them.
Quite impressed with her memory, she began naming all the trees in
Africa and then began to recall the names of all the trees in the world.
Lost in her thoughts, she carelessly stepped in the same hole in the
ground that had spoiled the gazelle's journey just the day before. But,
unlike the gazelle, the elephant's foot was so big and fit so tightly into
the hole that she could not easily get it out.*

*The elephant pulled and tugged but her foot wouldn't budge.
Those animals who where not too weak from hunger ran toward the
elephant shouting, "What is the name of the tree?"*

*Angrily, she pulled and tugged at her foot again and again until
at last she was able to free it from the hole. "What is the name of the
tree?" the animals shouted again.*

*"I can't remember," she said crossly, as she rubbed her sore foot,
"and I don't care."*

*The animals were too tired and too hungry to complain. Some
began to cry. They didn't know what to do. Then, a very young
tortoise said, "I will go and find the name of the tree."*

"You are too young, too small, and too slow," replied the animals.

"Yes," said the very young tortoise, "but my great-great-great-grandmother, the one who knew about the tree, taught me how to remember."

Without waiting for the animals to respond, the little tortoise headed out slowly across the great plain. Step by step she made her way to the place near the river in the jungle where the lion king lived.

The king was not at all pleased to see the tortoise and roared, "If you have come for the name of the tree, forget it! I've told it twice before. And I warned the gazelle and the elephant that I would not tell anyone else the name of the tree is Ungalli so I will not tell you."

The young tortoise politely thanked the lion for his time. As she walked out of the jungle she repeated to herself over and over, "Ungalli, Ungalli, the name of the tree is Ungalli." She crossed the great plain, saying over and over, "Ungalli, Ungalli, the name of the tree is Ungalli. Ungalli, Ungalli, the name of the tree is Ungalli." Even when feeling tired and thirsty, the young tortoise never stopped saying, "Ungalli, the name of the tree is Ungalli," because great-great-great-grandmother had said this is what one should do to remember. Falling to the bottom of the same rabbit hole that had tripped the gazelle and trapped the elephant, the young tortoise just climbed out saying, "Ungalli, Ungalli, the name of the tree is Ungalli."

None of the animals noticed as the young tortoise approached them. They were lying under the tree preoccupied with their great misfortune when she walked straight up to them and announced in a loud voice, "Ungalli, the name of the tree is Ungalli!"

The startled animals looked up. They saw the branches of the tree bend down so low that they could reach the wonderful fruit that was as red as pomegranates, as yellow as bananas, as orange as mangoes, as purple as plums, and as fragrant as all the fruits of the world.

The animals ate until their bellies were full. With great joy and merriment, they lifted the very young tortoise high up in the air.

They paraded around and around the tree singing and chanting, over and over, "Ungalli, Ungalli, the name of the tree is Ungalli," because they did not want to forget. And they never did.

Like the animals in the story, the woman who seeks to end her inner famine needs to find the name of her hunger, for it is only by naming her hunger that she can be fed. The tree in the story is a magical, mythical tree. It has fruit no one has ever seen, fruit that embodies the colors and scents of all fruits. So it is with the tree of life that can provide nourishment to the woman who is emotionally and spiritually famished. The nourishment she seeks comes from no food she has ever seen, for it is Nourishment with a capital N.

To learn the name of her hunger, she must journey back into the past from where she came, cross the great empty plains of her life, travel deep into the jungle of her mind, find the place near her river of feelings where her inner authority rules, and ask, "What is the name of my hunger?"

But it is not enough to simply learn the name of one's hunger. In order to be fed, a woman must remember the name of her hunger. She must keep it in the forefront of her mind, moment to moment, as she makes her way toward recovery from disordered eating. She must remember what it is she is truly hungry for every time she slips or stumbles into addictive patterns and reaches for a food that cannot feed her real hunger, every time she falls into the addictive trap of using food to soothe her aching heart or broken spirit. She must remind herself, "This is not what I really want. What I really want is love. What I crave is attention and acceptance. What I long for is creative expression. What I yearn for is a spiritual connection."

When a woman is steadfast in reminding herself over and over of what it is she is hungry for, when she patiently puts one foot in front of the other, keeping her awareness of her hunger in her consciousness, she will not forget. And because she does not forget, she will be able to receive the true Nourishment that life has to offer.

My experience tells me that, unlike addictions to substances, someone can fully recover from an eating disorder. An alcoholic places her entire sobriety at risk if she has one alcoholic drink, even if she has been in recovery for years. This is not necessarily the case with someone with an eating disorder. Once recovered, she can go through the rest of her life without having to struggle with food, fat, or dieting. Once she recognizes that her urge to eat when she's not physically hungry is a signal of a different hunger she needs to address, she can begin to discover ways of feeding herself the nourishment she truly desires.

6

Symbolism

Hunger as a Metaphor

For most of us, eating takes on meaning way beyond physical nutrition. It can be used as a substitute for love if we are feeling unloved. It can provide a kind of comfort, warmth, even security. This connection is easy to understand when you consider that as babies, our earliest experiences of being loved typically involved being held in our mother's arms while we were fed. This can be a very powerful association especially if, later on in life, we feel deprived of sufficient experiences where we feel totally loved or accepted. In order to recapture our earlier experience of feeling emotionally nourished, we might try to re-create it by feeding ourselves food and not realize that it is love we are really hungry for.

Eating can be used as a means of providing comfort and support at times when we are feeling sadness or pain. This is a relationship supported by many families and by our culture. We are taught that any pain should be removed as soon as possible, that it's a bad thing to experience. So when a child goes to the doctor and gets a shot, she is given a lollipop. Or if loved ones are feeling sad, we try to cheer them up by offering them something to eat.

Eating can be used to escape from uncomfortable feelings in much the same way that drugs and alcohol have been used and abused. If we are having a difficult time coping with confusing or conflicting feelings, we may discover that by starving, we are able to disconnect from our bodily sensations so that we can't feel what's inside, or we may discover that we can plunge into bingeing large quantities of food or eating small amounts of food nonstop whenever those feelings start to surface. You can't breathe freely with a too-full belly, and if you can't breathe freely, you can't experience your feelings.

Remember the last time you ate a huge meal, when you really stuffed yourself? Remember the sensation you experienced before the guilt set in? You might recall a numbing sensation, where all feeling was blocked out of your awareness and, at least for that moment, you weren't aware of the exam you had to take the following day, the fight you had with your husband, the job you dreaded going to.

For those who feel a pervasive sense of loneliness and emptiness, food can serve as a constant companion. Eating becomes something to do, a way of filling up the empty space in their lives by creating a sense of fullness in their stomachs. Others may starve themselves so they won't notice their loneliness. That way they won't have to take the risk of meeting new people or getting too close to others who they fear might reject them.

For many people, food is a means to communicate thoughts and feelings they don't know how to communicate directly. The child who experiences her diet-conscious parents as very controlling may put on weight as a means of saying, "You can't make me be just like you. I am my own person." Or she may become anorexic to "really show them" who is in charge of her life.

We all use food to one degree or another for reasons other than physical nutrition. It only becomes a problem when it becomes the only thing we ever do to cope. Then we become like "one-trick ponies," doing that same one thing over and over again to get love, to cope with emotional stress, to communicate our anger, to bear our sadness. A woman caught up in this cycle may experience herself as hungry, but she misinterprets this in all cases as a hunger for food.

Hunger can really be about much more than food. Hunger can be about the need for comfort and nurturance, the need for self-expression, the need for spiritual fulfillment. Any of these needs, when unfulfilled, can leave us feeling a certain emptiness inside. But when we interpret all hunger as a hunger for food, those other needs get buried deeper and deeper and never get taken care of.

To achieve freedom from struggles with food and eating, a woman must learn the language of metaphor. In the language of metaphor, hunger might represent a variety of feelings, needs, and desires. There are all kinds of examples of how our bodies speak to us in metaphor. A "pain in the neck" might really represent some nuisance or irritating situation in life that we need to take care of. We have all felt the need at one time or another to "get something off our chests." We have all felt "heartbroken" and had "gut reactions."

In order for a woman to recover from disordered eating she needs to discover the deeper meanings of her hunger, so that she can recognize that her desire to eat compulsively may be speaking to her about her greatest heart's desire that remains unfulfilled; her tendency to stuff herself may be an attempt to stuff down "unacceptable" or "troublesome" feelings; her need to eat continually may be a reflection of the constant emptiness she experiences in her life; her obsession with having zero body fat may reveal a desire to hide her curvaceous femininity.

Long, long ago in Japan there was a jolly old woman who lived alone in a little house halfway up a hill. She had a few chickens that gave her eggs, but not much more. She usually had very little food to eat and often went hungry.

One evening when she was making a couple of rice cakes for her meager dinner, the rice cakes fell off her kitchen table onto the floor and proceeded to roll out the door and down the hill. Propelled by her hunger, the woman ran after them.

Down, down the rice cakes rolled, picking up speed as they rolled along with the hungry old woman in pursuit, until they came to rest against a slab of rock. Laughing and breathless, the old woman reached down to get her rice cakes when a long, scaly, claw-like hand reached out from behind the rock and snatched them up.

She peered behind the rock just in time to glimpse a large creature scrambling away through a narrow opening in the rock. "My dinner! My dinner!" she shouted, as she hurriedly followed the creature while it scurried through a dark, narrow tunnel. The creature did not stop until it reached a large cave where it was joined by several more strange-looking, large creatures.

The old woman stopped short and took in the sight of these ugly creatures who had horns on their heads, enormous mouths that stretched from ear to ear, and three red eyes that were all staring at her. She realized that she was now in a den of the Oni, Japanese demons that lived underground and only came forth at night.

Because the old woman was so hungry, she became more angry than frightened as she watched the greedy Oni gulping down her cherished rice cakes. "Those are my rice cakes!" she shouted at them. "You have stolen my dinner."

The Oni just stared at her as they licked their claw-like hands. Then one of them said, "Did you make the rice cakes?"

"Yes, I did," the woman answered. "I happen to make very tasty rice cakes," she couldn't resist bragging.

"Well, come with us and make some more," the Oni said as he headed deeper into the cave. The woman followed him, for she was now more hungry than ever and couldn't resist the thought of eating *a meal. They went down through a maze of tunnels until they arrived at a cave where there was an enormous round cooking pot. The Oni dropped a few grains of rice into the large pot and filled it with water.*

"You'll need more rice than that," the old woman scoffed. The Oni just glared at her and handed her a flat wooden paddle. "Take this and start stirring," he instructed.

The old woman did as she was told, and to her amazement the whole pot was soon filled with rice. She made a huge pile of rice cakes for the Oni, taking care to eat some herself.

"I'm ready to go home now," she announced, "if you would be so kind to show me the way."

"Oh, no," snarled the Oni. "You must stay here and cook for us."

This was not at all what the old woman wanted to do, but when she realized she was surrounded by Oni and did not know her way home, she decided to keep her thoughts to herself.

The old woman proceeded to make rice cakes for the Oni while privately making plans to escape. She noticed that the water for cooking the rice came from a nearby stream, and she knew that the Oni did not like to cross water, so she figured if she could find a boat she would be able to escape. While she cooked and stirred the rice, she spotted an empty cooking pot that was a little bigger than she was and decided that it would serve very nicely as her escape boat.

The next day, while the Oni slept (for they were night creatures), the old woman put the stirring paddle into the empty pot and dragged it down to the stream. She hopped in and began to use the paddle to paddle herself downstream. But the sound of the dragging pot had awakened a couple of the Oni, and they rushed to the stream's edge where they shouted in rage.

The old woman paddled faster and faster as she noticed that the Oni were sucking up the water from the stream and swelling up like monstrous balloons. Soon the pot ground to a halt against the rocky bottom of the stream and fish flipped and flopped about in the now dry streambed.

"Here, have some fish!" the old woman shouted as she scooped up the fish and began to toss them at the Oni. The greedy Oni, who were always wanting more food, caught the fish with their claws, but when they opened their mouths to eat them, the water from the stream came rushing out and the old woman was afloat again, chuckling at her cleverness.

Eventually, the enormous cooking pot carried her to safety. When she came ashore, she left the pot but kept the magic stirrer and returned to her home on the edge of the hill where she lives to this day.

And she never went hungry again, for with the magic rice paddle, she was able to make as many rice cakes as she needed, and even have enough left over to share with her neighbors.

Stories such as this old Japanese folktale can help us move into the world of metaphor, where we can discover hidden meanings buried beneath the surface, where we can receive the clues that will guide us to freedom from our obsession with food.

The old woman, like so many of us, chased her food because she was driven by her hunger. What is the food that you chase? What might it symbolize? And what is the hunger you are trying to satisfy? For this woman, chasing her food led her to an encounter with hungry demons that lived hidden underground and had voracious appetites. You may recognize these demons as the ones you wrestle with within your own psyche, the ones that don't show their faces in the light of day but become ever present when the sun sets. What is it they are hungry for? What do they want you to feed them?

Stories such as this and stories such as yours are not to be taken literally. If you do, the characters and the events will seem too preposterous to contain anything of value. But if you can sink deeper into the stories, let them meander around in your psyche, you will discover the truth that they carry amid the tall tales, a truth that can reflect your personal struggle and help reveal solutions to your particular predicament.

In this story, the demons that live underground, in the darkness, were called Oni. What would you call your demons that hide deep in the dark crevices of your unconscious? Addiction to Eating? Loneliness? Fear of Rejection? Financial Insecurity? Self-Loathing? Not-Good-Enough? Never-Thin-Enough? What is it that haunts you, nags at you, holds you captive, wants you to feed it?

Imagine that you have a magic paddle that can create a limitless supply of food to feed your demon. What would that food be? What does your demon want to eat? What does it want you to feed it? Attention? Love? Money? Self-Acceptance? Your Rage?

As long as we interpret our nonphysical hunger literally, we will attempt to use food to satisfy it, and we will remain hungry forever. But when we can define our hungers and develop a deeper awareness of what we are hungry for, we can begin to seek the appropriate nourishment.

7

Feelings

Gifts from the Heart

Many people are afraid of their feelings, especially the so-called negative emotions. They are afraid they can't handle their pain, that it will overwhelm them. They are afraid that if they allow themselves to feel their loneliness it will last forever, that if they fully experience their anger they will do hurtful, destructive things. They attempt to ignore or keep under tight control all their "bad" feelings like fear, sadness, anger, and loneliness.

Women who struggle with disordered eating tend to be more frightened of their feelings than most. They have learned to mistrust their bodies and discount the body's most intimate way of communicating—the language of the emotions. To keep a safe distance from their bodies and feelings, they distract themselves with activities of all kinds and with constant thoughts of food. Anything but letting themselves feel. They live "in their heads," allowing their intellects to dominate, keeping their feelings at bay. Sadly, many fail to recognize that our feelings can provide us with some of the most powerful keys to self-knowledge and recovery.

This Vietnamese folktale, called "The Wonderful Pearl," reminds us of the healing that comes from exploring, rather than trying to control, our feelings. It teaches us that there are wondrous gifts to be found when we plumb the depths of our feelings, gifts that can help us with all the problems we encounter in life.

On the banks of the Mekong River, a long, long time ago, lived an orphan girl named Wa. Ever since she had first grown big enough to carry a basketful of rice upon her back, she had worked for the headman of the village.

All the villagers worked long, hard hours. And, just like everyone else, Wa was barely given enough to eat in return for her labor. She had to cut down tall trees, and when the rice was ripe, she had to peel the husks from dawn to dusk. Blisters welled up on her hands from all the cutting of wood and the coarseness of the rice husks made her palms itch and scale. Each night she gathered herbs to put on her raw, itching hands. Over time, she developed a great knowledge of the healing powers of herbs, and others in the village would seek her out for help with their wounds.

One day, the headman's messenger arrived and ordered Wa to guard the rice house, which stood on piles close by the paddy field. The rice house was filled with stores of rice, and the hungry girl longed to eat some, but she was ever mindful of the master's warning: "An evil spirit protects my rice. If you eat even one grain, the spirit will jump inside you. Then you will die and turn into a grain of rice!"

Paralyzed by her fear, poor Wa went hungry. In her dreams, she saw her master growing fat and rich from the stores of rice, while the villagers who toiled for him grew thin and sick.

One night, she was rudely awakened by a violent kick to her side. It was the headmaster's son who shouted, "You lazy pig! Fill this pail of water by my return."

Wa jumped up in alarm and ran swiftly to the river to fill it up. The waters of the river lapped softly at the girl's feet as she

*sighed and bent down to fill the pail. All of a sudden the waters
began to foam and sing, making her scamper back to dry land
in fear.*

*Out of the shimmering moonlit foam, a tall maiden appeared,
wearing a long, lustrous gown. She approached Wa and, taking her
trembling hand, said softly, "The Water Spirit's young daughter has
fallen ill. And our sprites say that you, Wa, are wise with herbs and
can cure her. Come with me and see her."*

*"No, no, I cannot," Wa cried out. "I must remain here to guard
the rice house. If my master were to find me gone, he would surely
have me killed."*

*"Wa, take mind not to anger us. The Water Spirit is more
powerful than the chief of your village. You will be punished by the
sprites if you refuse to come."*

*A pathway opened before her and the maiden led Wa down into
the watery depths. There she saw the sick girl who she had been told
was stung by a scorpion while playing at the water's edge. For three
months she had lain in a fever, unable to eat or sleep. Wa touched the
wound and told the sprites which herbs to collect. Three days after she
had applied the herbal remedy, the girl was well.*

*The Water Spirit was overjoyed and asked what Wa wanted as
a reward. Wa replied, "I wish only to be able to save my hungry
people, to do what I can to help."*

*The Water Spirit handed her a precious pearl, saying,
"Whatever your wish, this pearl will make it come true."*

*Wa thanked the Water Spirit and returned to dry land. Upon
her return, she recoiled in horror at the sight of all the bird tracks
around the rice house she had left unguarded. The birds had helped
themselves to half the unprotected rice!*

*Just then an old man passed by and said, "Where have you been
these last three months? Those thieving birds have stolen the master's
rice. He is searching for you and his rage is terrible."*

Wa sat down and cradled her head in her hands. She thought she had been gone only three days. She began to cry, soaking her thin dress with her tears. Just then, she remembered the precious pearl. She took it out and said, "Pearl, wonderful pearl, bring me rice to eat."

Suddenly, a great bamboo dish of rice appeared before her, filled with foods of all tastes and colors. Behind her a store of rice grew up three times higher than the master's rice house.

She took out the pearl again and said, "Pearl, wonderful pearl, bring me a house, a pair of oxen, and some hens." Almost in that very instant, a tall house on bamboo stilts rose up in front of her, with hens scratching the ground nearby. Next to it stood a pair of sturdy oxen.

The next morning, Wa made her way to the headman's house. As soon as he set eyes on the girl, he roared, "Here comes the worthless lump of oxen dung, the one who stole my rice. I'll have her fed to the tigers in the hills!"

"It was not my fault you lost your rice." Wa spoke up boldly. "But don't worry, I'll replace what you lost. Just send your son to collect it."

The headman's son snarled, "I'll take it now. And if you fail to replace it by a single grain, I'll bring your head back on a tray."

When Wa and the headman's son reached Wa's lavish house, with its huge store of rice, his jaw dropped open in surprise and his eyes nearly popped out of his head. "Take all you want," said Wa. "I'm going to the river to fish."

The sight of such wealth so impressed the man that he looked at Wa with new eyes. "I do not want your rice," he stammered, "I only want to marry you."

Wa only laughed. "Just take your rice and go," she said, "I can't stand to look at you."

When he made his way home and reported back to his father, the enraged headman summoned his guards to slay the girl and take her riches for themselves. But the good people of the village warned her of their master's plans. Once again, she took out the magic pearl and said, "Pearl, wonderful pearl, protect us from this evil man."

Suddenly a chain of mountains sprang up around the headman's house. He and his men were unable to scale the heights and were never able to bother the poor people again.

The wise, just Wa shared her wealth among the people, who never went hungry again, and she protected them always with her wonderful pearl.

Like Wa, a woman who struggles with disordered eating lives in a world filled with responsibility, duty, and deprivation. She is always hungry because there is no room in this world for how she feels and what she wants. Her life is controlled by the words of a "head" man who lives within her, an inner tyrant that drives her to do more, more, more and then refuses to reward her properly for her hard work.

It is the "head" man that denies her adequate nourishment, demands she watch her food carefully but not eat if she is hungry, instills in her a fear that if she eats even a tiny morsel, she will be taken over by the evil spirit of indulgence, and accuses her of being nothing but a "lazy pig."

When a woman who is seeking freedom from disordered eating goes to the river of feelings that runs through all life, she may be frightened when the waters of her emotions foam and sing. Like Wa, she may initially resist plunging into the watery depths of her feelings (by insisting that she has to watch over her food, instead) until she understands that the wrath of emotions denied can be great.

In the story, it was only when Wa went deep into the river waters, deep into the world of emotion, that she could heal and receive the wondrous pearl that would help her nourish herself, obtain abundance, grow in strength, and protect herself from those who would hurt her. In that same way, it is only when we allow ourselves to fully experience our feelings that we are able to receive the precious gifts they have to offer. By allowing ourselves to have a deeper relationship with our feelings, we can discover that each of our feelings holds a pearl of inner wisdom.

Anger can bring clarity and strength. When we let ourselves feel the full force of our anger, the clarity we receive can be amazing. When we recognize, "this is what ticks me off, this is why, and this is how I need things to be different!" we can experience the relief that such clarity can bring. A good relationship with our angry feelings can give us the determination to forge ahead, the strength to "stand our own ground," the energy and focus to let the world around us know what is and is not okay.

The paradox of fear is that by embracing it, you can transform it. What might, on the one hand, be paralyzing, can be transformed into something that brings forth trust and the courage to proceed. Denying or fighting with our fear can result in panic and stagnation. By embracing our fears, we can discover what we really need to feel safe.

With loneliness can come the gift of self-awareness. If you let yourself get to know your loneliness by being still with it rather than keeping yourself so busy running from it, you may learn why you keep others at a distance and how you do it.

Sadness offers the gift of healing and cleansing when we allow ourselves to cry. It teaches us compassion for ourselves and for others. Sometimes, situations that bring up a lot of sadness can provide us with the opportunity to heal past hurts and cry those "little girl" tears that weren't safe to cry "back then."

Jealousy can make us aware of what we want for ourselves, what we truly desire.

So, when a feeling comes knocking on your door, don't run and hide and pretend no one is home. Don't slam the door in her face and say, "Get lost! I'm busy and don't want to be bothered." Invite her in. Ask her, "What brings you here?" Get to know her.

Go with her. Thank her for her gifts. Treat her presence with honor and respect. For she is truly your friend and is there to help.

Feelings are like fluid waves of energy. Like the waves we see in the ocean, they come in, peak, and pass, come in, peak, and pass. They have a natural cyclical rhythm like the ebb and flow of tides, the waning and waxing of the moon. The flow of feeling is as natural as the flow of life itself.

Children seem to be more adept at letting their feelings flow through them. They find it easier to laugh from the belly, cry deep tears, howl with anger. They've not yet learned to be afraid of themselves, to be untrusting of their bodies, and to be obsessed with trying to make a good impression. Children live from one emotional moment to the next. Their emotional lives are unblocked. It is not unusual for a child to be sad and upset one moment and then to be happy and laughing the next.

I remember one time when I was feeling tired after a long day's work. I'd spent the day trying to do too much and, after a day of seeing clients, shopping, cooking, tending to the children, I wanted nothing more than to tune out the world around me and rest. Just then, my five-year-old daughter became upset about something and began to cry. I stopped what I was doing to console her, but she continued crying. Finally, I said, "If you're going to keep crying, go to your room and cry." And she looked at me and sniffled, "But Mommy, I'm just trying to get the last bit of tears out." It was one of those moments when I knew she had reminded me of something important.

To help us cope with our fear of our feelings we learn to block them out. We build dams to stop the natural flow. We create compulsive behaviors with food to distract ourselves from them. Rather than pay attention to feelings, rather than letting ourselves feel, we think about food and eating. Or exercising. Or working. After years of doing this, our awareness of our feelings gets pushed so far back behind the curtain of our obsessions that we lose touch. Our feelings become like aliens that mystify and frighten us. We don't recognize them, can't identify them or give them names. We can't communicate with them, can't make contact, can't cope. We're not even aware of them until they get so intense that they consume us. Then, our pain becomes intolerable, the loneliness feels like it's never going to end, our anger may push its way out in destructive or violent ways.

Pressure builds up inside of us as we live with our accumulated feelings over time. Physical tension, nervousness, irritability, stomachaches, headaches can all result from holding in feelings over years and years. How have you learned to cope with this pressure? Do you distract yourself by keeping very, very busy, by counting calories or pounds, by dieting, or by eating compulsively? Do you attempt to get some relief from the ever present tension by exercising, by bingeing and purging?

It is important to understand that it is not the feelings themselves that cause the bingeing and purging, the compulsive eating, the starvation, the obsession with food and fat, or the fat attacks. It is our attempt *not* to feel the feelings.

Picture yourself next to a large swimming pool. You are given a big beach ball and instructed to swim the length of the pool with the beach ball. For some reason, you get the idea that you are supposed to swim with the beach ball under water.

Can you imagine how difficult that is going to be? All of your energy and attention is going to have to go into keeping that ball submerged. What if the ball slips? It will most likely shoot up into the air, out of control, and you will have to scramble after it, using up even more of your energy and time. By the time you reach the other end of the pool, you may be exhausted.

Now, picture the same pool, same beach ball, same task. But this time you decide to swim across the pool with the ball on the surface, tapping it with one hand as you swim alongside of it. Imagine how much easier this is going to be! You can swim on your

back, turn somersaults, chew gum, sing songs, talk to people around
you, and still get across the pool using a fraction of the time and
energy you needed in the first scenario.

What I am suggesting is that we don't have to go through life
with our feelings stuffed down, always worrying about losing control of them. Stuffing down feelings takes up a lot of the time and
energy that might otherwise be spent having fun, doing interesting
things, and participating in relationships. Stuffing down feelings
and then having to worry about them slipping out of control can
lead to a life that has food as its central focus rather than the joy
of living.

An essential part of recovering from disordered eating
requires dropping judgments about feelings, developing an understanding that feelings are neither "good" nor "bad". There are no
right feelings or wrong feelings. Feelings just are. The only "negative" feelings are the ones that we can't accept in ourselves.

Feelings are not necessarily rational. Sometimes you can
make sense out of how you are feeling, but the understanding usually comes after you have fully experienced the feeling. If you try
to "make sense" out of the feelings before you have allowed yourself to completely feel their depth and breadth, you may find yourself confused or frustrated.

I remember a time during the pregnancy of my first child
when I was feeling very, very sad. But I could not find a reason
for my sadness. I had planned for this pregnancy and had wanted
this baby for some time. Yet I couldn't shake this pervasive feeling of sadness. So I went into my bedroom and decided to be
with my sadness until I discovered what it was about. It took
hours. My husband came in and asked what was the matter. I told
him I didn't know but I was going to find out by letting myself
feel whatever feelings came up. I just let the tears roll down my
cheeks and eventually I started to sob. I paid attention to whatever images entered my mind without censoring or judging them.

After a long while, certain thoughts kept reappearing and I realized why I was feeling so sad.

I discovered that although I was ready and eager to become a mother, I was feeling sad about giving up a lifestyle of freedom that I had cherished and so thoroughly enjoyed. I realized that in leaving the "maiden" phase of my life and by entering the "mother" phase, I would never again be so footloose and fancy-free. I would no longer be able to make decisions in my life without having to take into consideration the needs of another being.

By going into my feelings, I discovered that I needed to grieve the ending of this phase so that I could fully enter the next, without any resentment. I believe that had I dismissed my vague feelings of sadness or scolded myself for crying "for no reason," or stopped my crying by arbitrarily deciding that I had cried "long enough," I would never have reached the level of understanding that I did.

It is important to make a distinction between feelings and behavior. Behavior can be controlled. Feelings cannot. They have a life of their own. Trying to control feelings is like trying to swim up a mountain.

Unlike behavior, feelings cannot harm you or others. They can be uncomfortable and unpleasant, and at times they may be the impetus for hurtful behavior (if not expressed correctly), but they are not bad or destructive in and of themselves.

Feelings can cause trouble, however, if they aren't recognized or accepted. They are waves of energy that can either flow through us or get blocked. They do not just disappear. If we ignore our feelings or suppress them, they seem to take on a power of their own, and their expression becomes distorted or perverted in some way.

Something entirely different happens, however, when we let ourselves experience our feelings fully and totally without fighting them or trying to talk ourselves out of them. When we allow ourselves to be totally immersed in our feelings, we can experience something miraculous and wonderful: the feelings will pass. They will flow through and be gone. And we will feel the freedom to move on, without being encumbered or weighted down by them. This doesn't mean that they won't return, but once we become adept at riding out our feelings instead of blocking them, we will find that they pass more and more quickly, and with less and less effort and struggle.

When we stop seeing our feelings as the enemy, something that just gets in the way of doing what we think we should be doing, we can establish a different kind of relationship with them. As we make friends with our feelings, we can discover that they can be allies and guides in this journey we call life. They can lead us to a place of deep understanding about who we really are and what we truly want, a place we might not otherwise be able to reach.

Recovery from disordered eating depends upon creating a friendly relationship with our feelings, responding to them with curiosity, not judgment, and receiving the gifts they can bring.

A woman seeking to change her relationship with her feelings so that she can be free of disordered eating first needs to increase her awareness of her feelings so that she can sense their presence inside of her. She needs to learn about the different sensations she might experience and pay attention to where in her body she feels them. This will help her to distinguish one feeling from another.

Instead of jumbling up her feelings and describing them in vague terms, such as feeling "bad" or "upset" or "okay," she must learn to be more precise and specific. She needs to be able to recognize the sensation of anger, for example, and to notice how it feels different from the sensation of frustration or fatigue or irritation, until she gets a very clear sense of the different physical experiences the different feelings can bring.

Next, she needs to learn to accept her feelings, without judgment, without discrimination, understanding that there is no right way or wrong way to feel. Although some feelings may be more pleasant or seem more socially acceptable than others, no feeling is superior to any other. Different feelings bring different experiences into our lives and offer different lessons.

Finally, she needs to express her feelings in a clear, direct manner. This means if she is sad, an appropriate way of expressing these feelings is to cry or write in a journal. If she is angry, she might talk about her anger with a friend or the person with whom she is angry, or go in the shower and yell, or write a nasty letter that is not sent. If she is lonely, it might be most appropriate to call a friend or write a letter to someone she misses. Sometimes, she may not need to do anything at all but just be with the feeling until it passes. The point is that how she responds needs to fit with how she is feeling, so that she is not responding to each emotion with the same behavior: feeling sad? eat; feeling angry? eat; feeling lonely? eat.

Recovery from disordered eating requires an acknowledgment of how you are feeling and learning to distinguish one feeling from another. It requires an acceptance of *all* feelings without judgment. It requires an acknowledgment of the idea that feelings don't have to make sense, don't have to be liked, but, simply, have to be accepted. And finally, it requires some honest expression of how you feel, and a willingness to act with honesty and integrity.

8
Relationships
Singing the Truth

*This old African folktale is about a girl who lived in a village at a
time when life was very hard. The crops were not growing. Food was
difficult to come by. People had to trap birds, dogs, even lizards and
rats just to stay alive.*

*One day this girl was sent out to check on the bird snares.
When she returned empty-handed, the villagers said, "Where are the
birds? We are starving!"*

*"There was only one Tutu bird in all of the snares," she replied,
"and it sang the sweetest song I have ever heard, a song that filled me
with such joy, that I felt compelled to let it go."*

"You let it go?" they asked, finding such an act beyond belief.

*"We have no use for a girl like you!" the angry villagers yelled.
And in the throes of their rage, they dragged the girl out into the bush
where they built a small hut around her, a hut made of strong thorn
branches that had neither windows nor doors. There they left her.*

*The frightened girl cried and cried as she sat alone in the dark
hut, not knowing what her fate would be. When she had no more
tears to cry, she began to sing. She sang the most beautiful song, a
lament to the sweet-singing Tutu bird, whose life she had saved. She
sang this song over and over and over.*

When she stopped singing, she sat in the dark silence of the thorny hut and listened. She heard a little sound that was like a far-off bird cry and then a fluttering that seemed like wings, followed by the rustling of what might be a mouse. She looked upward to the top of the hut where the sound came from, and there she saw a small hole with a shaft of light coming through. She was surprised when a small fruit dropped from the hole and landed at her feet. It was sweet, juicy, and delicious!

It became quiet again, and the girl waited in the dark silence.

After a time, she heard the sounds again, and another fruit fell to her feet. When she glanced up she noticed the hole was a little bigger and she was able to see the Tutu bird hovering above. The girl thanked the bird profusely. Then the bird sat on the roof of the hut and sang the same sweet song that had compelled the girl to free her.

For many days it continued like this. The bird dropped sweet, juicy fruit down to the girl, the girl sang thank-you songs to the bird, and the bird sang ever so sweetly in return. Each time the bird sang, it made the hole a little bigger, bringing light into the hut.

At last the time came when the hole was big enough for the girl to climb through and she was freed.

To celebrate, all the birds of the forest joined the Tutu bird in making a great feast of delicious fruits and nuts for the girl and for the people of the village. The villagers who had been so cruel to the girl were surprised at how well nourished the girl looked, for they remained thin and miserable. They praised the birds and welcomed the girl back to the village, in hopes of benefiting from her good fortune.

But the girl refused to speak with them or to eat with them. She went off into the forest with the birds and was never seen again.

A woman's song is her truth. The expression of her innermost thoughts and feelings is the sweetest song she can sing and it should not be muted. Unfortunately, there are those that cannot appreciate the beauty of this truth or recognize its need to be expressed freely.

Many women who struggle with disordered eating fail to hear the sweetness of their own song because they are too busy listening to the singing of others, whether it be the voices of their parents, lovers or husbands, women friends, colleagues or classmates, or the chorus of the culture they live in. Rather than searching for the essence of who they are and expressing it in their own unique voices, they allow others to define how they should be, what they should look like, what they should do, what they should want. Unable to hear their own inner voices they feel a vague but ever-present sense of alienation that is hard to bear. Longing for a sense of inner connectedness and finding the estrangement from their true selves intolerable, they fill their minds with thoughts of food and they eat the way they live, as if in a trance, not conscious of what they truly want.

Because they feel so disconnected from themselves, they cling desperately to their relationships with others, hoping to get the attention, love, and support they are not able to give themselves. As they become increasingly dependent on these relationships to provide them with the nourishment they need, they become overly protective of the relationship itself. Cautious of anything that might be disruptive, they are quick to discard their own ideas and values whenever conflict arises. They see their own personal song as threatening to their relationships, as a nagging tune they must get out of their minds. And once again, they turn to food to distract themselves from speaking their truth, from daring to sing out loud.

Unbeknownst to those around them, these women are starving. By failing to respect and respond to their own needs, they become depleted rather than nourished in their relationships. They have become so adept at listening to the needs, wishes, and values of others that they have forgotten their own. Much of the time, they are unaware that they once had a voice that is now lost, a voice that could sing a song so sweet that it could fill their hearts with joy. And so they look for joy in eating or in losing weight.

To find her inner voice, a woman must recognize her need for self-nurturance, for a period set aside for quiet reflection. By learning how to take time out from her relationships with others and sit quietly with her own thoughts and feelings, she can be nourished. She can find her feelings, her values, her rhythms. She can hear the beauty of her song.

To be in a relationship with another in a way that nourishes rather than drains her, a woman must be able to listen to others without losing her own voice. She must learn to find a balance between her relationship with herself and her relationship with others.

In the ocean, the lobster and the eel are very close neighbors. The eel makes its home deep in a hole in the reef. The lobster lives at the mouth of this hole. With the lobster there to guard the entrance from intruders, the eel can live quite comfortably. The lobster, however, must remain alert not just to predators from without but from within as well, because eels eat lobsters. It must simultaneously keep one of its antennae pointing outwards and the other facing inwards.

Just as maintaining this delicate balance in awareness is essential to the lobster's survival, a woman seeking freedom from disordered eating must maintain a balance between her need to be in relationships with others and her need to remain true to herself. She must remain aware of her inner thoughts and feelings even while interacting with others. To do this, she needs to change the questions she asks herself. Instead of asking questions like

What will she think if I do this?

How will he react if I say that?

What do they think about my being here?

She needs to ask herself

How do I feel about what she just said?
What's my reaction to what he just did?
What's it like for me to be here with them?

In this way, she can continue to remain present and attentive to others without losing her sense of herself, who she is and what she values.

Most women feel deeply moved by the feminine principle concerned with harmony and relationships. They value the human connections they have with their friends, lovers, coworkers, mates, and children. The feeling of community, of being connected, of belonging, is an important part of every woman's sense of identity and self-worth. Striving to create nurturing, supportive relationships is an important aspect of a woman's life.

Valuing and appreciating harmony in relationships is one of the inner feminine's greatest gifts. Sometimes, however, a woman can over-identify with this priciple. In an attempt to create harmony and connectedness, she assumes total responsibility for her relationships, for making them happen, fixing what's wrong, making everything all right. It becomes she who does all the compromising, she who sacrifices what she wants to keep things agreeable, she who sings someone else's tune to keep the peace.

Many women who struggle with disordered eating find themselves surrounded by others who do not share equally in the responsibility for nurturing a relationship. These women frequently find themselves feeding and supporting others who do not feed and support them in return. They have women friends who talk but do not listen, coworkers who expect favors but do not give them, parents who criticize everything they do, husbands or lovers who try to convince them that they are out of tune whenever they sing a song they don't want to hear. Discouraged, they stop singing. No more beautiful songs of joy, sweet songs of sorrow, lively songs of change and freedom. They turn to food instead to give them the pleasure they once got from singing. And their relationship with food becomes the most important relationship in their lives.

For a woman to be free of disordered eating, she must bring the masculine principles of separateness and autonomy into her relationships. She must be able to say no. She must assert her individuality within the relationship and say, "That may be okay with you, but it is not okay with me. I understand you want me to do that, but it doesn't feel right to me. I don't share your perspective. It may not be important to you, but it's important to me. I feel differently than you do about that." Like the girl in the story, she needs to say no when others treat her poorly for not doing what they want and appear to value her only for what she can do for them.

In order to be free from disordered eating, a woman must realize the beauty of her song and refuse to sacrifice it, even in times of scarcity, even when others insist that she be silent. She must refuse to participate in relationships with those who do not value her voice and who would abandon her or imprison her for failing to destroy or silence it. She must beware of those who would punish her for not attending to their needs and who would refuse to nurture her if she sings freely. She must recognize that it is her song, the expression of the truth of who she is, that can nourish her and free her.

9

Power

Dominion versus Domination

I believe a key issue underlying all disordered eating is power. When I first meet with someone struggling with disordered eating, one of the initial topics of discussion is her sense of powerlessness. Typically, she sees herself as unable to chart the course of her own life, as a victim of forces beyond her control, subject to the wills of others, enslaved by her appetites. She presents a lot of evidence to substantiate her sense of powerlessness: her lack of "will power" for dieting, her inability to stop the binge-purge process, her lack of success in controlling her feelings.

Some professionals to whom these women turn for help also view them as powerless: victims of compulsive behavior, victims of dysfunctional families, victims of sexual abuse, etcetera who need to be told what to do (what to eat/what not to eat) rather than taught how to reconnect with their inner guidance, the wise voice deep inside of them. Others who attempt to empower these women become mystified and frustrated when their efforts are rejected and recovery is "sabotaged" time and time again.

It needs to be understood that it may not be a sense of powerlessness that is at the root of the disordered eating. It may instead be a fear of power. Fear of the power of one's feelings (especially anger), fear of the power of one's perception (especially when they see things differently than others), fear of one's intelligence and talent (when others might become jealous), fear of the power of one's sexuality (which may lead to advances from others they don't know how to handle). Fear of the power of being a woman.

Women who struggle with disordered eating are, more often than not, women with exceptional abilities. They have a highly developed sixth sense; they have the ability to see the invisible, to read between the lines. They become afraid of these abilities because they have received the message that these abilities are dangerous. So they become afraid of their intuition. They fear the power of the feminine.

When you look at their histories, it's easy to see how these women learned that their power was dangerous. One woman's earliest memory was of breaking a rock over another child's head in a fit of anger. Because a four-year-old has difficulty understanding the difference between feelings and behavior, she became convinced that her anger was harmful. Another woman tells a story of being attacked by the boys in her first grade class who threw snowballs with rocks in them at her. Earlier she had proudly demonstrated that she knew the answers that they didn't in math class. Yet another recalls feeling that her achievements were never good enough for her mother, who would subtly criticize her accomplishments. She learned to associate success with rejection. The woman who was sexually abused as a child by her loving father concluded that it was the power of her sexuality that caused the abuse.

Take some time to remember your early experiences with your personal power. Think back to when you were around four, five, six. Were you able to feel things others didn't? How did others respond when you described your perceptions? What about the times you felt that you did something well? How was that received?

Were there secrets you felt compelled to keep? In what way did you discover that the full expression of your power was considered dangerous? When did you first find it difficult to be yourself with all of your power and be in a relationship at the same time?

In order to recover from disordered eating, a woman needs to move into a new understanding of power, one which will enable her to be comfortable with her intrinsic power, one which will allow her to be in her power and participate in relationships with others at the same time.

There are two different kinds of power. The one with which most of us are familiar is the power of domination, or power-over-others. This kind of power is based on a hierarchy: top dog over bottom dog, winner over loser, strong over weak, rich over poor, big over little. This is the kind of power that has been used to run this world for the last several thousand years, since the advent of the patriarchy: strong country over weak country, rich over poor, humankind over nature, and male over female. It is the kind of power that most of us grew up with in our families.

Underlying the power of domination is belief in the concept of limitation, or what I call "the pie." Imagine that you and I are sharing a pie. If my piece gets bigger, then yours gets smaller. If you get more, then I get less. This belief creates an atmosphere of competition and suspicion. I have to keep an eye on you to make sure you don't get more and you have to watch me carefully so that I don't get the upper hand.

Most women have a difficult time with power because they have experienced only the power of domination. Within this system they see only two roles available when playing the game: the winner or the loser, the bully or the victim. They don't want to be the loser, but they are uncomfortable with being the winner. They don't want to be a victim, but they are repulsed by the idea of being the bully. So they refuse to deal with power altogether. They throw it away when it is given to them, and they do whatever it takes to diminish any sense of personal power that they feel stirring within.

Fortunately, a new kind of power is emerging into our awareness today. It is called the power-from-within or the power of dominion. Unlike the power of domination, the power of dominion has no hierarchical structure. It is based on equality. Rather than being based on a belief in scarcity or limitation, it is based on a belief in abundance, the assumption that there is enough to go around. This results in cooperation rather than competition. No one has to win and no one has to lose. That way, if I have something you want, all you have to do is let me know, and I can tell you how to get some for yourself.

The power of domination comes out of the patriarchal system of control and conquest that we have been living with for the last several thousand years. The power of dominion is more feminine. This does not mean that it is available only to women. Women, however, may have an easier time accessing it because they are somewhat more receptive to their intuition, to that process of looking within that the power of dominion requires.

When a woman can step out of the perceptual framework of domination and into dominion, she can have a whole new way of working with power, a whole new way of being in the world. As she begins to appreciate that her power can come from within without depleting someone else's, she can become more comfortable holding on to her power while she participates in relationships. She can allow herself to feel the power of her emotions and express them honestly and directly without feeling the need to attack others or put them down. She can allow for differences in opinion without getting trapped into power struggles over "who's right and who's wrong." Through her example, she can teach others with whom she has relationships that her becoming more powerful does not in any way diminish their power. When she no longer sees power as "bad" or dangerous, she will no longer feel compelled to keep her power in check by doing what she is doing with food: starving, eating compulsively, or bingeing and purging.

An old Swedish tale illustrates the difference between the power of domination and the power of dominion:

A long, long time ago, there was an evil wizard who lived in a magnificent castle high in the mountains. Surrounding the castle were beautiful gardens, filled with bright flowers and delicious fruits. Here and there throughout the gardens were statues of young maidens that were so lifelike one would have thought they were alive.

Alas, the sad truth was that these stone maidens were once as alive as you or me. Whenever the evil wizard saw a young maiden who appealed to him, he would use a clever disguise to capture her and bring her to his castle, where he would turn her into another statue to adorn his garden.

When the wizard tired of his collection of statues, he would prepare himself to fly off in search of a new victim. He dressed himself in the clothes of a nobleman, rubbed his lips with honey to make his words sweet, and sprinkled his face with May morning dew to make it appear gentle and kind. Then he wrapped himself in his magic flying cloak, which would enable him to fly high and low, over forests and valleys, and along pathways that led to the villages.

If he spied someone who pleased his fancy, he would spread his dark magic cloak on the ground. If a maiden stepped on it, he could immediately seize her and whisk her off to his castle high up in the mountains. The wizard's power, however, was limited in this way: the maiden had to willingly step on the cloak, otherwise he had no power to harm her.

One day while the wizard was in search of new prey, he spied a young maiden named Elsa walking down a path near her village. She had a berry basket in her hand, and her long blond hair glistened in the sunlight. It was the gleam of her hair that caught his eye, and the wizard swooped down onto the path and hid behind a bush. As Elsa approached him, he stepped out and spread his dark cloak on the path.

"Oh, beautiful maiden," he said, "your feet are much too dainty to walk on this rough, muddy ground. Allow me to serve you. You may step on my cloak."

"My feet are quite sturdy, thank you," said Elsa. "You should be more careful of your cloak. It will get quite muddy if you treat it like this." And she picked up his cloak, handed it back to him, and with a cheerful smile, headed on her way.

The wizard followed a short distance behind her, and schemed another way to entrap her. When he saw a large billy goat with sharp horns, he blew on his magic whistle to attract a swarm of bees which stung the billy goat about its face. The enraged goat butted at the bees, and when it saw Elsa coming down the path, it rushed to attack her.

The wizard hurried forward with his cloak trailing on the ground. "I will protect you!" he shouted, secretly hoping that she would step on his cloak in her haste to get away from the goat.

Elsa ignored him and ran round and round a bush with the goat after her while the wizard waved his cloak with no effect. When Elsa tripped, he threw the cloak down, hoping she would fall on it, but it was the goat that became entangled in the cloak.

The now furious wizard knocked the goat senseless, but not before it had torn a hole in the wizard's cloak.

When Elsa saw the tear, she felt sorry for him. "Your fine cloak is torn because you tried to save me. Let me mend it for you." And she plucked a thorn from a bush to use as a needle and a strand of her golden hair to use as thread.

The wizard was not appreciative of her offer, and when Elsa handed him the mended cloak, he complained that her stitching was

71

sloppy and irregular. When Elsa moved forward to see what irregular stitch he was referring to, she accidentally stepped onto the edge of the cloak.

In an instant, the wizard was transformed back into his cruel, ugly form, and they began to rise into the air, wrapped in the folds of his cloak. But the strand of yellow hair that had been used to stitch the tear in the cloak caught on the branch of a tree and held fast. Try as he might, the wizard could not untangle the cloak from the branch. While he struggled, Elsa slipped from his grip, slid to the ground, and ran as fast as she could down the path to her village. She didn't stop running until she reached the safety of her home.

The wizard returned to his castle, fuming with rage over his failure. That night, he could not sleep because his bedroom was so brightly lit that it hurt his eyes. At first he thought it was the moonlight that was ever so bright, but when he got up to close the shutters to his window, he noticed that there was no moon in the sky. The blinding light came from within his room.

He noticed that the light came from his cloak, from the stitches sewn with Elsa's golden hair. He rolled the cloak up tightly with the mended seam inside, but to no avail. The light shone through the folds of the cloth.

Night after night, the wizard was unable to sleep because the bright radiance lit up his bedroom and all the rooms in his castle. He tried to cut out the golden stitches, but could not remove them. Exploding with rage, he cursed the stitches, cut out the mended tear, and threw it out the window, only to find the seam back in place the minute he crawled back into bed.

In desperation, he flew down to Elsa's village in search of her home. When he found it, he rapped sharply on her bedroom window and called out to her to open it.

Elsa recognized his voice. She shivered in her bed but did not answer.

"Come here!" he demanded. "Take your thread out of my cloak. It shines with such a horrible light that I cannot sleep at night."

"Go away," Elsa retorted. "I will not come to the window."

The wizard threatened Elsa with great harm if she did not remove the thread, but she was not intimidated for she had learned from her mother that his only power over her lay in his magic cloak. When he realized he could not frighten her, the wizard tried to bribe her with a sack of gold, a farm filled with sheep, and all manner of fine things. Elsa remained suspicious and refused all offers.

At last the wizard gave up and returned to his castle in a very foul mood, during which he sat in his garden and scowled at his statues. "That stubborn girl has no fear of me. What can I do to demonstrate my power?" he wondered. In that moment, he decided to restore one of the statues to life so that Elsa could not doubt the extent of his power.

That evening, as the wizard prepared himself for bed, smugly convinced that Elsa would now be intimidated by his immense power, he noticed the light from his cloak had dimmed enough to allow him to sleep. But by the next day, it shone as brilliantly as ever.

Enraged, he flew down to Elsa's window, rapped on her window, and once again demanded that she remove the golden thread. "Don't you know that my powers of enchantment are far greater than your stupid hair? Remove the thread and there will be no more trouble for you."

"I think the seam is fine just where it is," said Elsa emphatically, and she refused to respond to his threats.

The furious wizard flew back to his castle on the mountain only to discover, night after night, that unless he released another maiden from his garden, the strange light would not fade. And so, one at a

*time, the evil wizard was forced to return an enchanted statue to life
in order to sleep each night.*

*When the last statue was gone, Elsa's golden stitches retained a
faint, steady glow — enough to warn the wizard that they would
flare up brilliantly if he ever used his evil powers again.*

The type of power the evil wizard wielded was the power of
domination. He was interested in having power over others, the
power to get his needs met regardless of how much pain he might
cause others. He had no qualms about using deception to gain
power. And he used bribes and intimidation in his attempts to
maintain his power. This is exactly the kind of power that most
women are all too familiar with and find abhorrent.

Elsa operated out of the power of dominion. She did not try
to dominate or control the wizard. Because she was aware of her
own power within, she was not easily seduced by flattery (you have
more power than I do) or intimidated by threats (I have more
power than you). Consequently she did not succumb to the fate of
the other maidens who had become frozen and lifeless in the face
of his power of domination. When, by accident, she was nearly
overcome by the wizard, it was her power of dominion, represented
by the thread of her golden hair, that saved her.

She honored her instincts and feelings, expressing them
assertively without putting the wizard down. She held her ground
and did not allow him to manipulate her into defending her position when he attacked her. She ignored his attempts to engage her
in an argument over whose power was greater.

The power of domination was symbolized by the dark cloak,
a costume often worn by villains who search for victims. Without
this prop, he had no power, just as those who use the power of
domination need their props of money, weapons, status, or aggressive body language to maintain their power over others. The power

of dominion was symbolized by Elsa's hair which grew out of her head. Because her power came from within, it could never be eliminated.

When a woman becomes assertive, like Elsa, she taps into a vast reservoir of power that lies within her, a sense of power that does not have to affect others adversely. She can then shift out of interpersonal relationship dynamics that are based on the power of domination into those that honor the personal power within each individual. She can let go of the fat that served to hide her power from others; she can stop the dieting and food obsessions that have kept her from recognizing and experiencing the full force of her personal power.

10

Nurturance

Mother as an Archetype

Once upon a time in a magical kingdom by the sea, there lived a beautiful princess who led a very enchanted life. Her father, the king, was an intelligent, creative man who spent most of his time coming up with new ideas for making things better. His kingdom prospered, and the people in the kingdom were pleased with him because their lives were so successful. He was a good father and loved to teach the princess new things. She learned her numbers and letters under his tutelage and often impressed him with her cleverness.

The young princess enjoyed spending her mornings with her mother, the queen, who was a very wise and loving woman. Often they would rise early and go to play in the forest with the gnomes and forest creatures. Sometimes in the afternoon they would visit nixies and mermaids down by the sea as they swam with the dolphins and fish. On special nights when the moon was full, they would visit the stars and dance with the fairies in the moonlight.

One day this enchanted life came to an end. The queen died. And the young princess was beside herself with grief. She cried and cried and cried. She wouldn't eat for days at a time. The king had his chefs serve up the finest dishes in an attempt to nourish her. This only made her angry.

Although he was a good and kind man, the king was frightened by the intensity of his daughter's feelings and tried to distract her from her grief. He invented elaborate playthings that eventually became the largest amusement park the kingdom had ever seen—but to no avail. He brought home other women to become her mother but the little princess rejected them all, as politely as she could. The king eventually gave up trying to console his daughter and went about his business of running the kingdom.

The years came and went. The princess no longer ventured beyond the walls of the castle. She could no longer see the gnomes, fairies, or nixies. She forgot the language of the forest animals and how to communicate with flowers and plants. Occasionally she would sigh when she heard the wind blow through the trees or cry when the moon was full. But she no longer understood these feelings or where they came from. Although her appetite returned, life held no passion. She ate, she slept. She ate, she slept.

The princess spent the rest of her time playing with her elaborate toys that became more and more sophisticated as she grew older. She continued to impress others in the kingdom with her bright and quick mind and the clever ways she used numbers and words. But she never regained her sense of life and vitality. She had long since recognized how it distressed her father for her to be unhappy, so she became quite adept at feigning joy and happiness.

On the morning of her twenty-first birthday she awoke and something was different. Colors seemed much brighter, her senses more finely tuned. Instinctively she ran to her window to behold the most beautiful rainbow she had ever remembered seeing. The scent of the roses and gardenias from the garden below wafted upward and she was captivated by their fragrance. She stood transfixed by the warmth of the sunlight on her cheeks. "I am alive!" she cried.

Throwing on a robe, she dashed outside and ran through her beloved forest, feeling its damp coolness on her skin and inhaling its pine and musty scent deep into her lungs. She ran until she came breathlessly to the ocean where, at the water's edge, she threw herself down on the sand and cried and cried and cried. "Where is my mother?" she cried as her tears mingled with the water from the ocean.

"I am here," a voice replied.

The princess was startled. The voice seemed to come from deep inside of her and all around her all at the same time. "Who are you?" the princess asked in amazement.

"I am your mother," replied the voice.

"Why did you not answer me before when I called for you over and over?" the princess asked, her natural curiosity returning as she expressed her frustration.

"Because," the voice replied, "in an attempt to cope with your grief, you shut down your heart and I could no longer reach you. Now you are open and awake so we can commune once again."

"Why did you leave me?" the princess asked.

"There were many lessons you needed to learn that you could learn best in my absence. From your pain, you learned compassion. Your anger gave you clarity and the strength you needed to endure. Your loneliness taught you self-awareness. By experiencing your greatest fears you learned courage."

The voice became quiet as the princess listened to the sound of her own breathing and the waves lapping on the shore. She felt a great sense of peace come over her. "May I come back and visit you here?" she asked.

The voice chuckled warmly, "My dear girl, I don't live here. I am everywhere. I am the sea. I am the flowers. I am the stars that shine at night. I am your breath. I am your tears. I am your Mother and I will never leave you."

Like the princess in this story, a woman who struggles with disordered eating experiences the loss of the Mother, that archetype of the feminine spirit that nourishes her, that keeps her deeply connected to nature and the rhythm of the earth, that supports her relationship with all that is invisible.

She lives in a world that does not perceive, honor, or celebrate whatever cannot be validated by the five senses. Emotions are regarded as troublesome or frightening. Anger is to be avoided, sadness eliminated as soon as possible. In order to survive in this world, she must deny or downplay them. She quickly learns that in order to please others around her, she must present a pleasant, happy face and hide any other feelings.

Although she can learn the ways of this world, and even be quite successful in her adaptations, she knows that it isn't real for her. She feels like she is just going through the motions. There is a certain emptiness in her life, an emptiness she tries to fill with food.

Her denial of her feelings is quite costly. She enters a self-imposed exile from the world of spirit and nature. As beautiful as her material world may be, it is barren, without passion or life force. And her longing to connect with her Mother never goes away. Her hunger is ever present, and insatiable.

Only when she opens up and allows herself to feel the full force of her emotions can she then experience her feelings as gateways to wisdom and guidance rather than as stumbling blocks to be overcome. She will no longer need to use eating or starving as a way to avoid feeling her feelings.

Only through the power of her emotions was the princess able to transcend the loss of her human mother and connect with the Great Mother archetype, the mother that is deep inside of her and all around her at the same time. For the woman who struggles with disordered eating, only by embracing the power of her emotions will she gain access to the guidance, support, and nourishment from her feminine spirit. It is the way she will come to know the Wise Woman who lives within her.

The woman who struggles with disordered eating might not have been orphaned from her mother like the young princess, but she has, for one reason or another, become disconnected from her internal mother, that aspect of herself that provides nourishment and compassionate guidance. By blocking and judging her feelings, she is unable to access the guidance and support she desperately longs for. She feels undernourished and attempts to fill up herself with food.

Some women whose eating is disordered felt disconnected from their external mothers at a very early age because their mothers were neglectful, abusive, or simply not available to them in the ways they would have liked. Others felt smothered and overwhelmed by mothers who were overprotective, controlling, and wouldn't allow them to make any decisions for themselves. Because of these experiences, these women were not able to develop adequate "inner mothers."

Their inner mothers are very young and, like most young mothers, very unsure of themselves. Their response to requests for nourishment can be very confusing. One minute they are overindulging, the next, withholding and judgmental. This gets played out in the woman's relationship with food, which acts as a metaphor for all nourishment.

These women need to develop an inner mother that is more mature, one that has a sense of balance and cares for them with a loving hand without being excessively indulgent; one that can assess what they really want and look beyond the pleas for chocolate to see if there is some hidden need that is not being satisfied. They need to cultivate an inner mother who supports instead of judges their feelings, who uses intuition and common sense to make decisions, who can bring into consciousness that which has been kept out of awareness.

Regardless of how deprived your childhood was or how completely you feel that your mother failed you, it is important not to place the blame for an inadequate or underdeveloped inner mother solely on the woman who gave you birth and raised you. Our society today has placed way too much responsibility for mothering on the shoulders of a child's mother without providing her with the support or resources needed to carry out such responsibilities. All of our mothers have had the unenviable task of raising a daughter to live in a patriarchal society that devalues her femininity. Most mothers are isolated, overworked, and undernourished. Consequently only a very fortunate few of us ever inherit a strong internal mother.

The past cannot be changed; the future is another matter. It is essential to recognize that you have within yourself the capacity to develop a strong inner mother, one that can provide you with the nourishment and guidance you need, not only to survive, but also to grow and flourish.

How do you do this? By treating yourself the way you would treat a child whom you care for very much. This means not scolding yourself whenever you make a mistake but, instead, re-framing your error so that it becomes a learning experience. Rather than saying to yourself, "What a stupid thing to do!" ask yourself, "Knowing what I know now, how would I do things differently next time?"

This means not judging your feelings or criticizing yourself for feeling jealous, hurt, or annoyed. Allow yourself the space to experience your feelings fully so you can learn from them.

This means following your intuition rather than blindly accepting others' perceptions or automatically doing what others want you to do in order to please them. It requires a certain vigilance so that you are constantly checking in with yourself, asking yourself, "How does this feel? Do I really want to do this?"

All this leads to the development of a highly conscious internal mother, one that can gather information based on the essence of who you are, and lovingly use it to guide you in your recovery from disordered eating and throughout your life. This is the mother that will never fail you because she will always be tuned in to what your needs are from one moment to the next.

11

Intuition

The Inner Seeing, Hearing, Knowing

Intuition is an invaluable gift from the feminine. It is the wise voice that tells us what to do, which way to turn, and if something is wrong. Unfortunately, most of us have been encouraged to disregard our intuition. We have been taught that the only knowledge that is valid is that which comes to us from the outside world through our five senses. We are taught to think, not feel, and to value only what is logical, what can be processed through the rational mind.

Intuition is a very different kind of knowing. It is perception beyond the physical senses that provides information that can be used for survival, creativity, and inspiration. It is not simply a mental process, but one which involves our bodies, our hearts, and our spirits.

The rational mind processes the information that it receives from the environment and forms logical conclusions. It offers guidance and direction based on this information. The intuitive mind has access to a much broader and deeper supply of knowledge. It taps into the creative forces of the universe that reside within and around us. It links us to a greater, more comprehensive understanding than what the rational mind can comprehend.

This is not to say that the masculine, rational mind should be rejected, but rather that it needs to be used in tandem with the intuitive mind. Your rational mind can be used to question (with curiosity, not judgment) the promptings received from the intuitive mind and to provide the focus and support needed for their expression.

Intuition involves a certain state of receptivity that is not necessarily passive, although it may appear to be so. When we are actively receptive, our awareness becomes more diffuse and we become more sensitive to subtle information from both within and without. While all of us have intuition, it is often called "women's intuition" because it is the feminine aspect of receptivity that comes into play.

Intuition cannot be commanded. It comes, seemingly of its own volition, when we are in a state of receptivity. That is why when we are struggling to solve a problem and can't figure out a solution, it is only after we have "slept on it" or have let go of the struggle that the answer comes, often in a sudden burst of insight.

Women seem to be naturally more intuitive because their biology forces them to remain connected to their bodies and their emotions. We have hormones that sensitize us to our feelings and instincts, and a menstrual cycle that mirrors the phases of the moon as a reminder of our connection to the universe, the bigger picture. Women may also be more intuitive because of the experience of being female in a patriarchal society. Since we learned very quickly that we did not have the physical strength to protect ourselves from the perils of domination such as incest, rape, or other forms of abuse, we had to become very adept at judging others, "reading between the lines," and seeing the invisible in order to avoid dangerous situations. We often had to make decisions before all the logical, rational information was provided and thus learned to develop a strong, intuitive sense.

In our culture, there has not been much support for intuitive knowing, and those who are closely connected to their instinctual selves through their intuition are often rejected by others. In my work with women struggling with disordered eating, it has become clear to me that this is exactly the kind of experience these women have had repeatedly in their lives. They found that if they voiced concerns or shared perceptions that could not be validated by their five senses or logical thought processes, they were either punished, ridiculed, or accused of "trying to stir things up," of being reckless, or courting trouble. They were told in no uncertain terms that their reality was wrong.

These women were so wounded by this rejection that they became distrustful of their feminine intuition, and their intuitive knowing was driven underground, into their unconscious, not to be acknowledged, even to themselves. In order to maintain the suppression of their intuitive faculties, they internalized the cultural judgments against this information with such statements to themselves as: "There is no reason for feeling this . . . I must be imagining things . . . I'm overreacting . . . I'm too sensitive. . . ."

And this became the refrain of their inner dialogue over and over again until they no longer believed they were capable of defining their reality. They lost their sense of an inner authority they could turn to for guidance.

They started to feel that something was terribly wrong with them but they weren't sure what. All they felt was this terrible pressure to keep their perceptions hidden from others, to hide their true selves, lest they be accused of being irrational (read: "crazy").

And they found that one of the best ways to ignore or quiet that inner voice was by distracting themselves with food, fat, and dieting. They learned to respond to "gut feelings" by putting food in their stomachs as though the rumblings came from physical hunger.

Recovery from disordered eating involves reclaiming your intuition, that inner authority that provides knowledge and guidance. It involves learning to use your intellect to support rather than discredit information obtained through intuitive channels. It requires that you develop an appreciation of the wise, compassionate guidance that is always available to you and that you choose to incorporate it consciously into your life rather than ignore it.

This old Russian story is about a king and queen who lived a happy life in a small kingdom long, long ago. The King took great pleasure in having his knights perform mock battles and compete in games of strength and skill. While this entertained him, he longed for an opportunity to go out into the world to test his skills and gain fame and fortune.

When word came to him of a cruel king from a distant country who was terrorizing a nearby kingdom, he decided that this was the opportunity he was waiting for. Leaving the Queen in full command of the country they had ruled together, he instructed his ministers to assist her in all things, and gathered up his finest knights to head out to help defend his neighbors.

He traveled on and on, through forests and over mountains until he reached the land where the enemy king ruled. There, he engaged in battle with the forces of the foreign king, only to be defeated and taken captive.

The King was hauled away and locked in among prisoners who were placed in chains and treated badly. By day they were forced to plow the fields. At night they were returned, exhausted, to the prison, where they were given barely enough food to sustain them.

Meanwhile, back in the small kingdom, the Queen governed wisely. Her subjects were happy and well and the kingdom prospered.

But the Queen longed for her husband, and when the months became a year, then two, then three, she feared he might never return.

When at last the King had found a way to send her a message, she was overjoyed. Although he was held captive, she knew now that he was alive! In his message, the King asked the Queen to sell off their castles and estates and borrow as much money as possible, so that she could deliver a ransom of gold and free him from the wretched prison.

The Queen thought long and hard about the message. She wanted to free her husband as quickly as possible because she missed him dearly and knew that raising such a large sum of money could take many months.

"Then if I bring the ransom gold myself," she thought, "this foreign king might seize the gold and imprison me, too. If I send couriers with the ransom, who will I know I can trust? And what if the ransom offer is refused or seized? This ruthless king may not want to ransom a prisoner—or he may be so wealthy he will laugh at our amount of gold."

The Queen paced her chamber in despair. "If I do as the King requests, when he returns home he will be poor and heavily in debt. The kingdom will be impoverished and our people will suffer."

She thought and thought until she could think no more. And then an idea came to her. She would journey to the distant land disguised as a vagabond minstrel, a lute player, and she would rescue the King herself. She did not know if her bold plan would succeed but she felt compelled to try it.

She was certain the ministers would be horrified by her idea and would detain her if they could. So she cut her long brown hair, dressed herself as a minstrel boy, and left a note that she was going on a journey. With her lute in hand, she slipped out of the castle at night, with only the light of the moon to guide her.

As the Queen journeyed she became thin and browned by the sun. The bright colors of her minstrel cloak became dusty and worn. In a little more than a month's time, she reached her destination.

When she arrived at the palace of the foreign king, she placed her lute in her hands and began to play and sing a mournful ballad that expressed a great longing for her heart's desire. So beautifully did she sing, all who heard her were touched by her lament. No sooner had the king heard her lovely song than he had the singer brought before him.

"Welcome, lute player," said he. "Where do you come from?"

"My country, sire, is far away across many lands. I wander from country to country, and I earn my living with my music."

"Stay here and play for us, then. When you wish to leave, I will reward you with what you wished for in your song—your greatest heart's desire."

After three days of charming the king with songs both merry and sad, the lute player came to take leave of the king.

"What do you desire as your reward?" asked the king.

"Sire, I would like one of your prisoners to have as a companion on my journeys. When I hear his happy voice as I travel along, I shall think of you and be grateful."

The king agreed to this and the Queen walked about among the prisoners. At length she picked out her husband and took him with her on her journey home.

During their travels, the King never suspected that this thin, sun-browned minstrel could be his Queen. When at last they reached the border of their own country, the King said, "Let me go now, kind lad. I am no common prisoner, but King of this country. Let me go free and ask what you will as your reward."

"Speak not of a reward," answered the lute player. "Go in peace."

The two parted and the Queen took a shorter way home, arriving back at the castle ahead of the King. She changed her clothes, putting on a splendid gown and a high silk headdress, to meet her husband.

The King greeted the excited throngs of people in the castle and then turned to his Queen and said reproachfully, "Did you not receive my message? I wasted for a long time in prison waiting to be ransomed! Now you greet me lovingly, but it was a lute player who rescued me and brought me home."

The Queen had planned to tell the King the reasons for her disguise in the privacy of their chambers for she feared that he would be angry she had not sent the ransom money. But before she had a chance to reply, a spiteful minister standing nearby said, "Sire, the Queen left the castle when news of your imprisonment arrived and she only returned this day."

At this, the King looked stricken and sorrowful. He turned away to confer with his ministers, for he had thought the Queen had deserted him in his time of need. The Queen returned to her chamber and slipped on her travel-stained minstrel cloak. She picked up her lute and went to the castle courtyard where she sang the verses to the songs she had sung in that faraway land.

Upon hearing the songs, the King rushed out to the courtyard, took the lute player in his hand and announced, "This is the lute player who freed me from prison! Now, my friend, I will offer you your heart's desire."

"I ask only your trust and love," said she, throwing off the hooded cloak and revealing herself as Queen. "And I beg that you hear my story."

A cry of astonishment rang through the hall. The King stood amazed, then rushed to embrace his wife. She then explained why she chose to use her skill as a lute player to rescue the King.

The King rejoiced in the wisdom and courage of the Queen and, in gratitude, proclaimed a seven-day feast of celebration throughout the land.

The queen in this tale represents our feminine intuition that, in an ideal land, rules over our lives alongside the king of our thought processes, logic. When faced with a dilemma that seemed unsolvable, when she had exhausted all logical possibilities, she received a novel idea that came in a flash of insight.

The queen trusted the idea that came to her even though at the time she was not quite sure it would work. But it was the plan that she *felt* was right, so she acted on it. To be intuitive is to be willing to risk, to be willing to step off not knowing for sure where one will land.

Intuition becomes available to us when we remain connected to our hearts. The queen trusted her feelings and allowed them to guide her toward the right decision; she missed her husband terribly and did not want to wait unnecessarily for his return. This motivated her to look within for a more creative solution rather than respond to the instructions she was given.

Unlike rational thought, intuitive promptings can be assisted by emotions. Because she let herself feel her longing for her husband, because she didn't deny her loneliness, the queen was able to allow her yearning for her husband to pour forth in her soulful song. Without engaging her feelings in her plea for her heart's desire, her song might not have touched the enemy king so deeply and her plan might not have been so effective.

The queen, as does our intuition, took in the bigger picture. When she followed the king's plan to its logical conclusions, she realized that it was too limiting. Even if it worked, there were drawbacks: the kingdom would be impoverished. When we tap into our intuition, we can connect with a broader fund of knowledge and expand out from a narrow, single-minded focus to one that recognizes the connectedness of all things.

The ministers represent the collective voice of our culture that distrusts the intuitive. The queen recognized not only that she would not get any support from them, but also that they would likely attempt to stop her from acting on her intuition. So she decided not to consult them and to avoid any confrontation with them altogether. She chose to maintain her sovereignty, to be her own person, and to follow her inner authority. We, too, need to recognize those who may scoff at our intuitive knowing and be prepared to pay them no mind, to do what we need to do anyway.

The woman who seeks to free herself from the prison of disordered eating must become receptive to the inner promptings of her intuition. She must listen within, reclaim her intuitive perspective, and appreciate its wisdom.

This means paying attention to her body signals ("gut" feelings) and instincts every day. It means respecting her impulses and hunches. It means honoring her feelings and insights by using this information for guidance.

In order to access your intuition, you need to be in a state of receptivity. Take time each day to be still, to do nothing, to focus on "being" instead of "doing." Let whatever thoughts and feelings come up enter your awareness. Take notice of any images or ideas that keep recurring.

Honor your emotions. Let your feelings flow through you without judgment. Focus on how you are feeling rather than what you "should" be feeling. Any blocked emotions or hidden feelings will interfere with your intuitive faculties. It is important that you get to know your different feelings and the different places in your body where you experience them so that you won't confuse certain feelings such as fear, for example, with intuitive promptings.

Drop the judgment. Instead of criticizing any messages you receive from your intuition, you need to question them with curiosity, messages such as: "I wonder why I don't want to go to work? What is it about being there that bothers me? Why does it affect me this way? How would I want it to be different?" Whenever you ask questions with curiosity instead of judgment, you are invoking guidance.

Check in with yourself. Rather than asking, "What will she do if I say this?" "How will he feel if I do that?" "What do they think about my being here?" you need to ask, "How do I feel about what she said?" "What's my reaction to what he just did?" "What is it like for me to be here?" All too often we look to the outer world for cues to guide us when the answers lie within.

Be patient with yourself. Reclaiming your intuition is a skill that may take some practice. It may take you awhile to recognize your intuitive guidance because it can take many forms. Sometimes you will get a very clear yes or no to a question. Other times it will be a vague uneasiness about a certain situation. It can take the form of a sudden inspiration to act in a certain way, a nagging thought, a long forgotten memory, or a dream.

Keep a journal of hunches, insights, and impulses that you suspect are intuitive promptings. Pay attention to events as they unfold, that bear out or substantiate these inner messages. Although your intuition can take many forms, it is never wrong. After awhile, it will become clear to you what your intuition feels like.

There may be times when you choose to take a chance and follow your intuition even though others in your life may criticize your actions. You will quickly discover that when you follow your intuition, you feel more energetic and powerful. Things just seem to flow. When you don't follow your intuition, you begin to feel stuck, helpless, and powerless. Everything seems like such a struggle.

A woman's intuition can never be irretrievably lost. Even if it has been buried beneath years of neglect and denial, it can be recovered by looking within and listening. Even if it has weakened and atrophied through years of disuse, it can be strengthened by acting upon its advice.

Always remember that at the very center of your being is a wise, compassionate woman who offers constant guidance. She is longing to be heard. And if you listen, she won't steer you wrong.

12

Dreamtime

The Journey Within

This old English story is about the value of dreams.

There was once a poor peddler who lived a simple life in a country village. He did not have much other than a small cottage with a large cherry tree in back. The cherry tree was encircled by a vegetable garden in which he grew most of the food for his family.

One night the peddler had the most incredible dream. He dreamed that he went on a journey to the London Bridge, and when he arrived at the bridge, he found a sack of gold. This dream was so vivid and seemed so real that it stayed in his thoughts long after he had awakened. He was so consumed with the images from this dream that late in the afternoon he announced to his wife, "I had a dream that I found a sack of gold under the London Bridge. I need to leave for London immediately to seek my treasure."

"You must be mad!" she exclaimed. "You can't just go off here or there because you dreamed there was gold to be found. You must stay here and provide for me and your family." But the peddler was insistent, determined as he was to seek his fortune. So his wife was left with no choice but to pack him some food and wish him well on his way.

The journey was a long one for he had to travel many dusty country roads by foot. Eventually the weary peddler came to the city of London, and with a little direction from kind passersby, he arrived at the bridge of his dream.

Alas, there was no gold to be found.

Nevertheless, the determined peddler remained at the bridge for days, ever hopeful that his dream would be realized.

On the eve of the third day, the peddler found his food supply running low, along with his optimism, and he thought, "What a fool I have been to follow my dream." As he was gathering his jacket and knapsack for his return trip home, a man from the inn across the bridge approached him and said, "I have been observing you from my room across the way and have noticed you have spent three days underneath this bridge. What are you doing here?" When the peddler told him about his dream, the man laughed. "I, too, have had ridiculous dreams! I once dreamed that I traveled to a small, modest cottage in a country village. Behind the cottage was a large cherry tree encircled by a vegetable garden. There, buried beneath that cherry tree, I found a sack of gold."

The peddler scarcely had time to thank the man and bid him good-day. He rushed home, dug underneath the cherry tree and found a sack of gold. And he, his wife, and family all lived quite well for the rest of their days.

Like the peddler in the story, we live in a society that does not place much value on dreams. When children have nightmares we say, "It was *just a dream*," as if to imply that there is nothing more to it. We speak of someone "being a dreamer" when we disparage her lack of accomplishment. As children we are admonished at school for "daydreaming." The idea that dreams provide access to an extraordinary source of information regarding our past, present, and future is not widely recognized.

In ancient societies, dreams were thought to hold all kinds of powerful and mystical qualities. Some believed that dreams were messages from the gods and goddesses, a key to unlock the mysteries of the universe. Others held that dreams actually provided a path into an entirely different world, just as real as our waking existence. Shamans of many cultures looked to dreams for revelations of future events while indigenous healers the world over relied on dreams for the wisdom to treat distress and disease.

In our modern Western culture, dreams have come to be associated with the "unconscious" mind, the deeper aspect of the self that normally lies hidden beneath the surface that we present to the outside world. Many psychotherapists work intensely with dream interpretation in the belief that dreams provide a "royal road" to self-exploration. The dream is viewed as a symbolic representation of the real thoughts, true feelings, and most heartfelt desires of the dreamer. However, many people, especially those drawn to the "harder" sciences, scoff at the notion that dreams have any meaning at all, considering them instead to be nothing more than "neurological static."

The great challenge of dreams is that to really be able to appreciate them, you have to be able to understand dream language. Dreams do not speak to us in the language of waking life. A dream is much like a poem or a painting or a story that bypasses our conscious mind and speaks directly to our soul by evoking certain thoughts, feelings or images that resonate with something deep inside of us. Dreams, like art, speak to us in symbol or metaphor, and do not follow the same direct, linear, logical thought processes we are accustomed to in most of our waking life. The metaphors found in poems, dreams, and fairy tales affect us on imaginative and emotional levels, not just on the intellectual level. If we try to relate to them from simply the literal, intellectual level at which we are most accustomed to thinking, we will not be able to discover or experience the more subtle and infinitely more complex meanings they have to offer. If we limit ourselves to literal interpretations, our dreams will just seem "weird" or be frightening. We won't understand them or won't *want* to understand them and will tend to dismiss them altogether, depriving ourselves of a chance to find the "gold."

The unconscious mind is like a vast sea of life's experiences, memories of the recent and distant past, possibilities for the future. The conscious mind is nothing more than a tiny island in the middle of that vast sea. For our limited conscious mind to be able to comprehend the immense knowledge available to the unconscious mind, this knowledge must be condensed into symbols that contain layers upon layers of meaning. This is done through the use of metaphor. Metaphors transform raw impulses, patterns, or instincts found in our unconscious mind into forms that can be assimilated by our conscious mind. One symbol, one word, one image found in a dream can contain an immeasurable amount of meaning for the dreamer.

When we learn the language of dreams, the language of metaphor, a whole new world opens to us. We develop a deeper connection with our inner selves, receive information for guidance, recover meaningful memories, and discover sources of inspiration and resources for healing. A dream can tell you where you are, where you have come from, where you need to go, and what you need to get there. Dreams often show us what we have overlooked or avoided in our daily lives; they often reveal feelings, thoughts, or attitudes that may be most helpful to us in our quest to become more conscious of who we are and what we want, to become more whole and complete. If, for example, in your dream you are horrified to discover that you forgot to put on clothes when you went to work, your dream may be revealing to you fears of being exposed or of feeling vulnerable in your job, fears that you might have been ignoring and may need to question or explore.

In order to receive the messages sent to you from your unconscious via the dream, it is important to recognize that the objects, characters, events, and locations in your dream are multidimensional *symbols*, not simply concrete representations of things, people, and places that may or may not be familiar to you. Dreams are much more dramatic in their presentation of images and ideas than our daily thoughts are. They tend to shock us and to exaggerate things in their attempts to get our attention. Unfortunately, many people get so frightened by the dream images they receive at night or by their behavior in their dreams, that they do their best to forget their dreams and lose an opportunity to understand their fears, an understanding that can lead to healing. They do not recognize the amoral nature of dreams and judge them according to waking life standards, failing to realize that dreams cannot hurt anyone. For example, if you dream of violently attacking and killing a security guard outside an art gallery in order to steal a painting, your dream is not telling you that you are a homicidal maniac with tendencies toward kleptomania. It may be, instead, trying to tell you something about the anger you are not expressing in your waking life. Instead of judging your behavior in the dream, it may be more useful to ask, who might you be angry at? Is there someone in your life that is keeping you from being creative?

In a dream, any figure might represent a person in your life or a part of yourself that you disown, that you don't want to acknowledge or accept as part of who you are. Upon careful analysis, you may discover there is a part of yourself (your inner security-oriented, authoritarian voice) that you want to get rid of in order to proceed with a creative project.

The relationships we witness and experience in our dreams tell us deep truths about the relationships among our many selves.

We are much more complex than we realize and have a whole array of characters that exist within our psyches. There are some aspects of our selves that are familiar and with which we feel comfortable identifying, such as our responsible, supportive, caring, practical selves. But there are other aspects, such as our creative, carefree, self-confident selves that may seem alien and yet other aspects that are downright distasteful, such as our irrational, critical, dissatisfied, self-indulgent, angry selves. It is those parts of our selves that we don't recognize or don't like and try to disown that often show up in our dreams, calling out to us, trying to get our attention. They may appear in a dream as dark, hostile figures trying to break into your house or as a pack of wild dogs chasing you, or as a couple of demonic creatures that are holding you hostage.

In dreams, male figures can tell us about our inner masculine, and females about our inner feminine. How the males and females are relating in a dream can indicate the nature of the relationship between our own inner masculine and feminine, between our logical, outwardly focused, independent, goal- and achievement-oriented self, and our emotional, intuitive, relationship-oriented self. Does one aspect feel threatened and dominated by the other or are they "in love" and working together as a team? If you dream, for example, of having sex with your best friend's husband, who is a financial consultant, this does not necessarily indicate any sexual feelings toward this person, but may depict a deep movement within yourself toward union with the masculine side of yourself that handles your financial "affairs."

Dreams about our mothers and fathers often tell us a lot about the parts of our mothers or fathers that we have taken in unconsciously and made parts of ourselves. At the same time, dreams might give us insight into our relationship to our mothering or fathering natures as well as to the archetypal concept of Great Mother or Our Father. Children or babies in dreams often represent our inner children, our vulnerable, undeveloped selves.

Dreams about animals often speak to us about our more instinctual nature.

When a woman is trying to understand the deeper nature of her struggle with food, her dreams can provide her with valuable clues to what she is really hungry for, what her unfulfilled desires are, what inner conflicts she is trying to resolve through her body size, what feelings she is trying to stuff down with food, what her fears are. Dreams can reveal, often very poignantly, in what way food, fat, and eating serve as metaphors in her waking life. They can show her what aspects of herself she wants to disown and how she uses food or dieting to keep them hidden. Dreams can also give instruction about what steps to take, what skills she needs to develop, what inner voices she needs to listen to, and which of her inner resources she needs to call upon.

Patty, a flight attendant struggling with compulsive eating, tells of a dream where "my two older children are flying first class to Hong Kong and I am upset because I am not on the flight." This piece of the dream was very revealing to her because she recognized it was a dramatic depiction of the deprivation she feels as a result of giving first class treatment to others in her life and not getting any in return. Her dream expressed her frustration over not being able to get away from her responsibilities and go on vacation.

The dream continues:

"My older kids are off to Hong Kong and I am riding in a convertible with my twin baby girls. The shuttle crash-lands in front of us and explodes. There is debris all around, but I manage to protect the twins and we are able to get away unscathed."

Patty made a connection between the openness of the top-down convertible and how vulnerable and unprotected she felt having two new babies to care for. The explosion of the shuttle illustrated further how vulnerable she felt when her child-care arrangements fell apart the day before.

"The twins and I go to this Chinese restaurant and I get extremely angry at the waiter and start screaming at him that he can't tell me what to get, that I want to pick what I order and that he has no business telling me what to order because I pay the bills. And then I pick up a chair and break it over his head."

The restaurant setting was a clue to Patty that these feelings of frustration and vulnerability were related to her food and eating issues. She recognized that at a Chinese restaurant she was trying to get the "food" her older children were getting in Hong Kong. The angry outburst suggests the inner rage she experiences when a part of herself—the waiter who waits on everyone—does not allow her to choose what *she* wants. The dream is directing her attention to her anger (hitting her over the head with it) and her need to express it so that she can consciously choose what she wants rather than use her compulsive eating behavior to distract her from feelings of deprivation, vulnerability, frustration, and anger.

Your inner dream maker can be your best guide through difficult situations. It often presents a dream story that moves one step ahead of the story you are living in your waking life, beckoning you on, urging you forward in uncovering the truth of all of who you are. With its own unique language of images, plays on words, and emotional states, it can teach you, paradoxically, to "wake up" to parts of yourself that you were not aware of or not using most effectively.

Tricia, a young woman who had struggled with bulimia for years and was on the threshold of recovery, reported this dream just before her final binge-purge episode:

"A woman is chasing me into the woods with a knife and is trying to kill me. She gets me to drive her to the woods under false pretenses and to my surprise starts to chase me. I'm really scared. Then, for some reason, I stop running and angrily say to her, 'It's not going to be this way. This is dumb! I don't want to be here. I have other things to do and I'm going to take you home.' I drive the woman (who is now complacent) home, but I see that she has a long, steep driveway and I think, 'I'm not going out of my way because I have a lot to do.' I say to her, 'I'll drop you off here' (at the bottom of the driveway). Then I kiss her on the cheek and drive away to do what I need to do."

Tricia immediately recognized that the woman in the dream represented her older sister who, since childhood, had treated her harshly, with hostility and criticism. Not too long ago, she had discovered that her binge-purge episodes inevitably followed instances when her sister had put her down or rejected her, or moments when Tricia *thought* about being judged by her sister. The dream showed her how she would run into the woods of her unconscious (by bingeing and purging) whenever her sister attacked her or whenever she feared being persecuted by her sister's judgment.

In this dream, however, instead of continuing to run, she became angry and stopped running. She realized she had other things she wanted to do in her life, and she didn't want to remain unconscious about how she felt or what she wanted. The dream revealed to her how expressing her anger over being treated this way could stop this process of running away from her true feelings.

On a deeper level, Tricia recognized that the woman in the dream also represented the part of herself that treats her the way her sister does, that ambushes her with excessive criticism and harsh judgment whenever she doesn't do what she "should" do or doesn't do something as quickly or as perfectly as it "should" be done. This is the "cutting" part of herself from which she seeks refuge in her unconscious bulimic behavior. The dream's message to Tricia is that it doesn't have to be this way, she doesn't have to stay in the woods. By experiencing and expressing her anger, she can return to the "driver's seat" of her life, bring this disowned critical part of herself home, set limits on what she is willing and not willing to do, and do it in a firm but loving way.

Dreams often give us clues that help us solve mysteries that baffle our more logical, conscious mind. They can present images that will unlock repressed memories and activate healing processes.

Cynthia had been hospitalized for anorexia as a teenager and never fully recovered from her eating disorder. As a young adult, she remained terrified of becoming fat and frequently purged her meals. Although she had been in therapy in the past, she remained unclear about what the deeper issues were that had triggered her anorexia and continued to be mystified about why she continued to struggle with disordered eating. The following dream provided Cynthia with the insight she needed that ultimately led to her recovery.

"I'm in my living room wondering when my husband is going to come home. I'm very irritated about this lady next door. 'She's slutty,' is what I tell myself. Now she's at my door, flirting with my friend's boyfriend."

This piece of the dream prompted a discussion about Cynthia's feelings about her sexuality and about how she doesn't trust it and how it sometimes disgusts her.

"When my husband comes home, he brings three guys with him. I've got to make them all dinner right now. They all pile in the kitchen surrounding me in the fridge. I can't figure out how I'm going to feed them all with what little food I have."

The dilemma about food in the dream resonated with Cynthia's fear of her own ravenous nature and her feeling that there is never enough to satisfy it. She began to suspect that there might be a connection between her relationship with food and her feelings about her sexuality:

"One man is fat, hairy-faced, short, and crude. One man is slimy, tall, skinny, and evil. One man is not really seen, even invisible. I can barely see him. He's nice. I pull out a bowl of something and start cooking. I'm overwhelmed and just when I feel like giving up, they all dive in and chow down on what I've cooked."

Cynthia recognized that the tall, skinny guy looked like a former boyfriend who, she found out later, had sexually molested her five-year-old sister. Talking about him and her feelings over what he did brought up old feelings. She had always felt tremendous shame about being with a boy who could molest her sister. When she was a "skinny" anorexic teenager, she was identifying with the behavior of her boyfriend, saying without words, "See, I'm just like him—perverted in my sexuality." The fat, hairy man represented her "crude," animalistic, sexual nature that she had associated with the "evil" acts her boyfriend committed against her sister. Her fear of becoming fat was connected with her fear of becoming sexual. The "nice" guy represented the positive aspects of her sexuality that she could "barely" see.

It is significant that the dream takes place in the kitchen, a place of transformation, where raw food is "cooked up," where raw instincts can be transformed into something palatable that can be consumed and digested by the conscious mind. In interpreting her dream, Cynthia could see that the starving guys were all the different aspects of her rejected sexuality that were wanting to be fed, that were wanting to become conscious. The process of trying to feed them food was overwhelming because, no matter how much she fed them, it was never enough. What these disowned parts of herself needed to be fed was attention so that she could be freed from the obsession with food and fat, an obsession whose purpose was to keep these aspects out of her awareness. Her dream presented her with a drama that would bring them that attention, her very own version of "Guess Who's Coming to Dinner?"

When a woman is struggling to recover from some form of disordered eating, it is important for her to remember that food is a metaphor and that through the process of understanding that metaphor, healing occurs. While dreamwork can be helpful in finding the often elusive meaning of that metaphor in particular dreams (by revealing the symbolism of food, what fat means to us, or how we use eating to express, suppress, or distract ourselves from certain feelings), it can be of even greater value when we learn the dream language.

When we begin to pay attention to our dreams and learn to interpret them, we become familiar with the language of metaphor. This helps us to recognize how metaphors operate in our waking life. We begin to see, for example, that food is a metaphor for emotional nourishment and that we tend to eat when we are hungry for attention, affection, or appreciation. We begin to see more clearly how stuffing ourselves rapidly with food is a frantic attempt to stuff down those feelings that are threatening to surface. We see how fat represents insulation from hurtful comments, protection from unwanted sexual advances, or protection from other people's jealousy.

Before she can decipher her dreams, a woman must first learn how to catch them. Even though everyone dreams, many women don't remember their dreams. Learning how to catch a dream can sometimes take concentrated effort. Dream images are usually fleeting, and often some special care needs to be taken in order to remember them.

The best time for dream catching is during that early state of reverie, when you are not quite asleep nor quite awake. If you get up too quickly or let your mind race immediately to those things you need to do once you are awake, images from a dream can be quickly lost. So take a moment to fix on any words, thoughts, or images that linger from the dream world.

The next thing to do is to record them immediately. It takes only moments to lose a dream. It is best to keep a dream journal and pen near your bed to jot down your dreams. Often just intending to record your dream of the night before and preparing the materials to do so, can elicit a dream memory. Even if you are not able to remember a complete dream, make note of any words, images or feelings that come to mind. In time, you will be able to describe your dreams more clearly. When recording your dreams, it is best to record them in both the first person and the present tense, as though they are happening while you are writing. For example, "I am driving down this dark road and the man sitting next to me is smoking a cigar." This helps you maintain the immediacy of the dream.

If there is a certain problem you want help with, make a mental note just before falling asleep at night, to ask for a dream that will give you the insight or guidance you need. Whatever your struggle happens to be with food, fat, or eating, ask for a dream that will reveal the symbolism of food, what fat means to you, or what feelings you are trying to express or suppress by eating. Ask for help in discovering the underlying issues you need to resolve or the attitude that will be most helpful to your recovery process. You may not get a dream immediately, it may take weeks, but when you do get the dream, there is a good chance you will recognize it as the one you asked for.

When it comes to interpreting dreams, there are no specific techniques that will give you the "answers." By experiencing many dreams and using your imagination to discover what certain things mean and what associations they have to your waking life, you will develop confidence in your intuition. You may want to get a book on dream symbols as a starting-off point, to help you get used to thinking in terms of symbol and metaphor. But it is important to understand that there are no right and wrong interpretations. Your dreams are *your* dreams, and are as unique as your fingerprints.

Although dreams can present many traditional archetypal symbols, those ancient, fascinating, often intense images (such as the Witch, the Queen, the Moon, the Mother) that speak to the human experience and have meanings that are common to various cultures, most dreams have very personal meanings that you must discover yourself. This discovery process is often very different from the analytical thought processes we are used to, where we quite deliberately string together ideas that build upon each other and lead to logical conclusions. Rather than using logic and sequential thinking to determine what the dream means, it is usually more helpful to mull about the dream images and feelings, letting the meanings emerge. What or who do they remind you of? When have you felt those feelings before? What sensations do they evoke? How is this related to what is going on in your life? Do they speak in any way to your feelings and concerns about food? Ask more specific questions without demanding immediate answers. If there are characters you recognize in the dream, ask what qualities do they have in waking life? How would you describe them? What do the objects in the dream symbolize? For example, ask yourself, what do I think of when I think of the ocean, driving fast, big teeth, the color red, chocolate chips, empty boxes, fish, baldness, etc.? What feelings do certain settings in the dream evoke? When have I felt like that before? If they are familiar settings, ask what was going on in your life the last time you were there. How are the males and females getting along? Is there conflict? Balance? Does the dream in any way speak to your struggle with eating, food, fat, body image? How does the dream end?

Instead of actively chasing the meaning of a dream, be receptive. Let an idea about the meaning of a dream come to you. When you ask questions, allow whatever answers come forth to speak to you, even if they don't immediately make sense.

Sharing your dreams with someone who is not too quick to tell you what they mean can be very helpful. Often in describing the dream or in explaining what certain things, characters, or places mean to you, you will discover even deeper meanings. I have one friend who I call first thing in the morning and we share the dreams we had the night before, and I have another friend I walk with in the morning and we often talk about our most compelling or interesting dreams. If you are in therapy, sometimes an entire session can be spent analyzing one dream or dream fragment which can reveal an enormous amount of information for guidance and healing.

While the content of a woman's dreams can be very valuable, the real treasure, as shown in the story of the peddler, is found in the process of following the dream. When a woman starts listening to her dreams, to her inner voice, she discovers that her truest source of knowledge comes from within. The answers to her life's struggles and dilemmas can be found by exploring her own personal experiences and feelings, not by adhering to the opinions and standards of outer authorities.

In the words of Cynthia, "I never realized how important my dreams could be. It amazed me how much information I could get from one little piece of a dream, just by writing it down and looking at it. But most of all, my dreams have helped me to trust my body, because by seeing how all this information was coming from inside myself, I could see how to trust my inner self and my body signals."

13

Moontime

Reclaiming the Body's Wisdom

Recovery from disordered eating calls for a new way of relating to our female bodies, one that honors and values what they have to offer us. It requires that we appreciate what it means to come into the body of a woman.

One of the aspects of being a woman that has been most hidden, denied, and devalued in our culture is the menstrual cycle. Since we live in a society that has suppressed the feminine in all of us, it is not surprising that a woman's relationship to that part of herself that is the most profoundly feminine is so often associated with feelings of shame, loathing, or pain.

We need to embrace this aspect of our being so that we can reclaim the deep wisdom that it can bring, the inner knowing that helps to keep us connected to the rhythms and pulse of life. The following story is one I wrote for my daughters to provide them with a new way of understanding the menstrual process, one that is different from the current perspective our society offers us. It encourages celebration and appreciation of menstruation as a special link to emotions and the wisdom inherent in nature's cycles.

Once upon a time when all people lived peacefully on the earth, there was a young girl named Tanya who lived in a small village at the edge of the woods. One day, Tanya was sitting on a mat weaving a new basket. She was becoming a very good basket weaver and had already woven quite a collection of harvest baskets for gathering the vegetables and flowers from her garden, When she stood up to reach for some grapevines to add to her basket, she noticed a little spot of blood on the mat where she had been sitting. This frightened her and she immediately ran to get her mother.

"Oh," said her mother when Tanya told her about the blood, "this is nothing to be afraid of. This is a very good sign."

Tanya looked into her mother's face and saw her eyes dancing with joy. Her mother smiled and whispered excitedly, "This means your moon power is coming! It is now time for you to go to Auntie's and learn women's earth magic."

Taking Tanya by the hand, her mother led her to Auntie's cottage at the far edge of the woods. No words were spoken when Auntie greeted them. The two women looked at each other knowingly and smiled at Tanya.

Tanya loved visiting Auntie. She had an enchanting, magical place, filled with wondrous treasures: silks and beautiful beads, exotic feathers, amazing seashells, and incredible crystals and stones of all shapes and colors.

Auntie gave Tanya a stack of bright red cloth pads and a bowl made out of red clay. "Take one of these," she said. "As more blood flows, the pad will soak it up. When it is full, rinse it in this bowl with some water from the stream near your garden. Then take the water in the bowl and use it to water your plants."

"More blood?" asked Tanya. "Does this mean I am hurt?"

"Oh, no," said Auntie, reassuring her. "All girls get this flow when it is time for them to become women. It is Mother Nature's way of letting them know that they are ready to learn about the woman power that flows within them. And every month, the flow will return to remind them of their power, in case they forget."

"What is this power? How would someone forget their power?"
Tanya asked.

"We will talk more later," said the older woman. "First, I want
you to take one of these baskets and gather some herbs in the woods."
She instructed Tanya to collect some blessed thistle, chamomile, and
lady's slipper flowers, some blue cohosh, false unicorn, and marsh
mallow roots, a bit of cramp bark, and some mountain raspberry
leaves.

Tanya was pleased with the task and quickly forgot about her
concerns. She loved wandering in the woods collecting roots and
flowers, and she had learned what these plants looked like and where
they lived when she was still quite little. She tucked one of the new
pads in her pants, and with a moss basket in her hand, she headed
out into the woods.

It was late in the afternoon when she returned. Auntie had a
kettle of water heating in the kitchen. They prepared the herbs and
put them in the hot water to steep. Auntie gave Tanya a cup of the
hot herb tea and said, "Sit down and drink this. We have much to
talk about."

"Oh, yes," said Tanya, feeling much more curious than afraid.
"Tell me about woman power."

Auntie sat back in her wooden rocking chair and began to
speak, "Mother Nature gives her children many gifts so that they may
experience life fully. If you understand and care for these gifts, they
will grow in power and your life will be filled with much beauty and
happiness. These gifts can take many forms, just as people can take
many forms. But there is one gift whose form is the same for all who
are female. It is the gift of the Flow which comes every month. The
Flow is a gateway for entering the great river of feelings that runs
through all life. It will carry you into the deep waters of your
emotions where you will receive the power that comes with trusting
your heart, the power to know when you truly know something.

"When a woman is about to enter her moontime, she becomes very, very sensitive. It is the time when she feels things the most strongly; the time when her ability to see the invisible around her is the sharpest; the time when her dreams and visions are the most powerful. It is a sacred time."

Auntie then leaned forward and looked at Tanya and spoke these words of caution, "As with any power, if it is not treated with care and honor it can become very destructive. Some women stop listening to their feelings. They throw away their ability to see the invisible and they quiet the voice that speaks to them from within."

"Why would anyone want to do that?" asked Tanya.

"Because," replied Auntie, "sometimes they are afraid to speak their truth because others around them might not like what they have to say. So they act like things are all right with them when they are not. They say yes to things when they want to say no."

"And then what happens?" asked Tanya.

"At their moontime, when they are most sensitive to their truth, they are unable to lie to themselves any longer and the river of feelings that had been dammed up throughout the month comes bursting forth in a torrent of hurt and anger.

"A woman in this situation can say and do some very hurtful things. Those around her cannot understand why she has such strong feelings about things that seem so small because they don't know that she has held back her truth for so long. And the woman forgets about the power of being in her truth. She thinks something is wrong with her. And she calls her gift the curse."

"Oh," said Tanya, "is that what you meant by women forgetting about their power?"

"Yes," said Auntie, pleased that the young girl seemed to be understanding so quickly. "And that is why it is important to honor this gift from Mother Nature, to trust your feelings, to listen to that inner voice, to know that you truly can see the invisible."

Auntie poured Tanya another cup of tea and continued. "When it is your moontime, your powertime, you need to spend much more time with yourself, your thoughts, and your feelings. It is a time to go within yourself. If you spend too much time with others and become too busy with the outside world, you will become resentful and grumpy. You may find that you get belly cramps or backaches."

"Why is this?" asked Tanya.

"Because Mother Nature is calling you to go within. There is a time for being busy outside yourself and a time to be still and go within. Whenever you fight the natural rhythms of the Moon and the Earth and your body, it can be very uncomfortable, even painful.

Tanya nodded her head in understanding and Auntie continued, "When you are in your moontime you will need more sleep than usual. It is very important to know this. You will receive many very strong dreams from the Dream Maker. They will be dreams for healing and dreams for guidance. You need to pay attention to them."

"And now," said Auntie, noticing that Tanya had drained the last few drops of her tea, "would be a good time for you to enter that dreamspace. When you wake in the morning, I will fix you a nice breakfast and we can talk about your dreams."

And so, Tanya curled up in Auntie's big feather bed, pulled a large silk blanket up to her chin, and fell asleep.

How might your relationship to your body, to your feminine self, be different if your introduction to your menses had been like Tanya's?

Take a moment to recall your earliest experiences with your menses. Were you caught by surprise, or did you know what to expect from your body? What were you taught and how? Were you taught that it was something troublesome, painful, disgusting, dangerous? Were you taught that you were better off ignoring it, as though it weren't happening? How did you interpret what was said (or not said) to you? What implication did you get about what it means to "become a woman"?

How did you feel? Were you frightened, ashamed, or excited? Did you have conflicting feelings?

What messages did you get from society at that time? How was "having your period" handled at school? What did it mean? How did the girls or women in your life respond to it? How did the boys or men react?

Think about the messages you still get from society today. Look at the messages the media give. Are women's menses discussed openly, in a matter-of-fact way, or is there much vagueness and innuendo? Pay attention to advertisements of tampons, pads, douches, vaginal deodorants. What do they suggest?

It is not surprising to find that the onset of menstruation often coincides with the onset of disordered eating. Many girls first show signs of being preoccupied with fat and weight around the time of their first menses. That is the time when their bodies are beginning to change, to follow a deeper, more primitive set of guidelines that they cannot control. They may not realize that most girls experience a significant weight gain sometime during the year preceding their menarche. It is the body's way of accumulating the fat necessary for processing progesterone, the hormone essential to menstruation. If these girls are already living lives where they feel as though they don't have much power or control, they may start dieting in response to this weight gain to give them some sense of being in control.

Feelings about what it means to become a woman and issues of feminine sexuality begin to surface at the time of menarche. If a girl's first palpable impressions of being a woman are not favorable, if she is afraid of her sexuality, she may try to suppress her fears by eating compulsively or she may turn to dieting to distract herself from her concerns. A desperate attempt to stop the tide of maturity can herald the beginning of an ongoing battle with her body, a seemingly endless cycle of weight gain and loss that she can only view as evidence of her flawed personality, her lack of "willpower".

So we find that, just as ancient societies had special rituals for girls at the onset of menarche to celebrate this rite of passage into womanhood, our modern society also has a ritual for adolescent girls to mark their entrance into womanhood. It is called dieting.

Women who struggle with disordered eating often report that when they are premenstrual, they have the most trouble with compulsive eating. They complain that it is during this time of the month that they crave certain "bad" foods and are unable to control their behavior.

These women deplore the onset of their menses because of the extreme mood swings they experience at this time. They find themselves withdrawing from, or overreacting to certain situations. They are easily overcome with fits of rage and tears of frustration. They assume something is wrong with them.

Our society, which has long been out of touch with the deep rhythms of nature, supports this misperception. Certainly there must be something wrong with them if they can't control their emotions or eating behavior when it is "that time of the month." There must be something wrong with them if they act and feel differently when they are ovulating.

We have a nice, neat diagnosis for categorizing such behavior and explaining it away. We call it premenstrual syndrome, PMS. It is a disease.

Because of these cultural attitudes, it doesn't occur to these women to question their feelings and cravings to see what their bodies are trying to tell them. It doesn't occur to them to look deep inside and ask what might be going on. Instead, they curse their menses for messing up their diet plans, for causing such erratic behavior.

Imagine if we women understood our bodies to be reflections of the cycles found in nature. We would recognize that the waters in our bodies follow a rhythm as sure as the change in seasons, the ebb and flow of the tides, the waning and waxing of the moon. If we honored the inherent wisdom of our bodies, we would learn to listen, to treat them with respect instead of judgment, and to experience them as sacred messengers that bring us information about our physical needs, our innermost feelings, and our individual internal rhythms.

PMS would come to mean "premenstrual sensitivity," the time of the month when all veils of illusion would be lifted and the truth would be most accessible. All those lies we'd told ourselves and others throughout the month would be revealed so that we could no longer act in ways that were contrary to our deepest feelings. It would be an opportunity to do some emotional housecleaning, restore our integrity, wipe our slates clean, and start anew, just as our bodies shed the linings of the uterus and start to prepare for new beginnings.

If you find yourself eating more when you are premenstrual, recognize it as a signal indicating that you need to listen carefully to your body so that you can determine whether you are eating in response to physical or emotional hunger. It is a time to pay particular attention to your physical sensations so that you don't confuse the activity in your uterus with your physical hunger signal. Use your heightened sensitivity to lead you to the truth of what and how you are feeling.

It may be a natural part of your monthly rhythm to eat more just prior to your menses and less during your menstruation. If this is the case, you may experience a slight weight gain during your period which is lost once your period is over. It is not unusual for a woman's weight to fluctuate throughout the month, just as the moon grows into fullness and then wanes into darkness.

If you are accustomed to eating compulsively when confronted with strong feelings, you may find yourself eating more when you are premenstrual because this is the time when emotional sensitivity is the greatest. Instead of fighting those emotions and stuffing them down with food, use this time as an opportunity to gain greater access to your feelings and to develop a deeper understanding of those feelings that might be triggering disordered eating behavior. Tendencies toward extreme mood swings or emotional overreaction are signals that there are feelings you have been suppressing throughout the month.

Once you learn to respond to your feelings by acknowledging, accepting, and expressing them assertively throughout the month, instead of by eating or dieting, the level of the intensity of your feelings when you are premenstrual will diminish. In time, you will come to welcome your menses and the gift of awareness that they bring.

14

Sexuality

Embracing the Feminine

When I was a young girl, growing up on the island of Guam, I was told a Chamorro legend that captured my imagination and kept me endlessly fascinated. This legend was first told to me by Doja, an old Chamorro woman who lived with my family since before I was born.

A long, long time ago there once was a young girl named Sirena who lived in a small island village at the edge of the ocean. Sirena was a happy, carefree child and spent much of her time singing and splashing where the mouth of the river opened into the sea.

As she grew, so did her love of the sea, and she would seize any opportunity to slip away from her chores and dive into the ocean waters, playing in the waves and singing her favorite songs. This annoyed her mother who tried in vain to teach her to sew, to cook, to sweep, to wash. She scolded her time and time again, "Sirena, you spend too much time playing in the ocean and too little time with your chores. You need to learn what a girl ought to know."

Her mother's words had little impact on Sirena and she continued her love affair with the sea. One day her exasperated mother said, "I absolutely forbid you to go swimming when I send you out on errands. You are to return directly home so that you will have time to complete your chores before nightfall."

Sirena was not a bad girl and she wanted to be a respectful daughter. Her intention certainly was to obey her mother as she headed down the dusty trail toward home, but she got no farther than halfway before she smelled the intoxicating scent of salt air and heard the murmur of the waves lapping the sand, calling her name. Before she knew it, her longing for the sensual caress of the sea overwhelmed her and she found herself once again immersed in the water, losing all sense of time.

When Sirena returned home at dusk, dripping wet, her mother flew into a rage and said, "You are a worthless, irresponsible girl! Worst of all, you refuse to obey your mother. If you love the ocean so much, so be it. May you spend the rest of your days as a fish!"

Luckily, Sirena's godmother was nearby and overheard the tirade. She understood that when a curse is spoken with such strong emotion, it has the power to be binding. "She may be your daughter," she said quickly, "but she is my goddaughter and therefore only half of her is subject to your curse."

In tears, Sirena ran to the water's edge, seeking the solace only the sea could give her. As she submerged herself in the water, she felt a change come over her body and was startled to find the lower half of her body covered with glistening, opalescent scales. Her legs had transformed into a long, undulating fish tail with a wide, graceful fan at the end. With her new tail, Sirena was thrilled to discover she could glide through the water with an ease she had never known before.

Sirena was never to be seen by her family again. Some say, however, if you listen very carefully on days when the sea is calm and the air is still, you can hear her singing among the waves. And if you are lucky enough to find yourself walking along the seashore when the moon is full and the tide is in, you just might catch a glimpse of her combing her long black hair in the moonlight.

While the legend of Sirena held great fascination for me as a child, it was only as an adult that I recognized how poignantly it spoke to my emerging feminine sexuality. The mermaid is an archetypal image that represents a woman who is at ease in the great waters of life, the waters of emotion and sexuality. She shows us how to embrace our instinctive sexuality and sensuality so that we can affirm the essence of our feminine nature, the wisdom of our bodies, and the playfulness of our spirit. She symbolizes our connection with our deepest instinctive feelings, our wild and untamed animal nature that exists below the surface of our personalities. While the mermaid can plunge to the watery depths of the feminine unconscious, she can also surface to sing her songs and have her voice heard. She is able to respond to her mysterious, sexual impulses without abandoning her more human, conscious side.

When a woman can trust her instinctive sensuality and sexuality, balance her conscious desires with her unconscious impulses, remain true to herself, and feel proud of her womanly body, she is embodying the archetype of the mermaid. Unfortunately, mermaids are hard to find these days. They exist mostly as enchanting but mysterious, faraway images in the minds of young girls.

Why are so few women able to be mermaids, comfortable with their bodies and their sexuality? Why are we frightened of or repulsed by our sexual nature? Why do we reject the most womanly aspects of our bodies? What happened to the girls who dreamed of becoming mermaids?

When a girl begins to become a woman, one of the first tasks she encounters is to learn to deal with the arousal of her sexual energies. Most of us are ill-equipped for this task, given the constraints of our culture, which tends to educate us about female sexuality as seen through the eyes of the patriarchy, where sexuality is equated with lust and women are portrayed as sexual objects, trophies, or prey. Little attention is given to the role of love or matters of the heart and none is given to the sacredness of the sexual act.

Just when she is beginning to experience her own sexual awakening, a girl is confronted with the reactions of others to her budding sexuality. Her sexual development is earlier (some begin to menstruate as early as nine or ten) and is more obvious than boys'. The growth of a girl's breasts is witnessed by all her classmates and the messages a girl gets in a society preoccupied with breast size can be one of the most traumatizing aspects of an adolescent girl's life. She usually does not have much time or privacy to develop a *subjective* view of her sexuality, to discover her own sexual nature, as seen through her own eyes and defined by her own experience. Any efforts to discover the true nature of her sexuality are undermined by the subtle and not so subtle messages about female sexuality she receives from school, from family members, from traditional religion and politics, from the music she listens to on the radio, from the TV shows and movies she watches, and from the magazines and books she reads.

Rather than delivering messages that inspire awe, respect, and reverence for her sexual nature and the mysterious transformation that is occurring in her body, these messages can be demeaning and alarming, and instead may provoke fear, shame, and loathing of her new womanly shape.

At school, boys tease girls who are "flat-chested" or have "big boobs," girls are ridiculed for having "big butts" or "thunder thighs." All of a sudden their bodies are up for scrutiny, as boys feel free to critique how they look, and they discover that their popularity is based more than ever on their physical appearance.

How girls are expected to respond to their own sexual instincts can be confusing. They encounter the double standard of the patriarchal power structure that calls boys who have sex "studs" who gain social power from being sexually active but calls girls who have sex "sluts" whose social status is at risk because of their sexual behavior.

Being popular seems to become more important than anything else, and they learn to focus on their *desirability* rather than on their *desires*. How they appear to others becomes more important than how they feel, than what they want or don't want. Fulfilling their desires, responding to their sexual appetites, can diminish their stature with others.

The media, which inundate us with imagery of how a beautiful girl or woman should look and provide us with only one acceptable body type (large breasts, narrow hips, thin thighs, flat belly), can have a tremendous impact on those who are looking for guidance on how to be more desirable. When a girl is learning about her sexuality from outside sources, she is easily influenced by the magazine, TV, and movie industries' distorted images of what female sexuality *looks* like, images that have nothing to do with what female sexuality *feels* like.

At home, a newly developing adolescent girl is often confronted with her parents' unresolved issues about feminine sexuality. If her father is threatened by the power of women's sexuality, he may make disparaging comments about certain parts of her body or her weight; if he views women as possessions, he may become overly protective and hostile toward boys who express an interest in her; or if he feels uncomfortable about his own sexual feelings, he may withdraw his physical affection. Brothers, especially those who are insecure about their own identity and personal power, can be especially merciless in their taunts about their sisters' physical appearance and in their use of sexually demeaning language. When an adolescent girl notices that the males in her family are uncomfortable with the outer signs of her emerging sexuality, she may reject her own changing body. She may use food to numb feelings of rejection and inadequacy or to alleviate the pain of being unacceptable.

Some mothers may experience envy toward their daughters' youthful, attractive bodies and become critical and competitive with them when they enter puberty and discover their sexuality. Compulsive eating or self-starvation may become a way for these daughters to distract themselves from feelings of confusion, estrangement, or anger. Other mothers, in an attempt to help their daughters adjust to this new phase in their lives, respond only to the dangers associated with their daughter's sexuality, dangers they know all too well from their experiences as women in a patriarchal society: sexual abuse, rape, incest, sexually transmitted diseases, and the shame and burden of unwanted pregnancies. Their fears can get transmitted by comments about the nature of male sexuality (boys only want one thing), through angry tirades over sexually provocative clothing, or by an uncomfortable silence or stiff body language whenever the topic of sexuality is raised. If they have learned to spurn their own sexuality through dieting or eating compulsively, this becomes a powerful model for their daughters desperately trying to cope with the pressure of defining who they are as sexual beings.

Regardless of the messages from her mother, an adolescent girl soon finds out on her own that she must defend herself from unsolicited sexual attention and invasive sexual advances from boys and men, whether they are strangers, relatives, or friends. More often than not, this occurs long before she has developed the assertiveness she needs to set boundaries. And so she may turn to food and fat to insulate, protect, and hide her sexuality. Or she may begin to diet and count calories in a vain attempt to reclaim the girlish body that no one noticed, that caused her no problems.

The wonder of her sexuality, her sacred connection to the natural forces of the universe, the awesome power of her body's ability to create and sustain life, the importance of her own sensual desires are banished from her awareness as she struggles to find her place as a woman in our culture.

In early adulthood, when these girls are attempting to establish meaningful relationships or sexual partnerships, they have already become separated from the beauty of their sexuality. They see themselves as unattractive and therefore not entitled to their sexuality. They find support for their beliefs in the media, which use images of thin, scantily clad female models in a state of orgasmic ecstasy (head thrown back, lips parted, eyes half shut) to sell everything from motorcycles to hand lotion to food products. In the absence of other sexual images, the viewer gets the message that *this* is what feminine beauty and sexuality are all about, and in order to feel the beauty and power of her sexuality, she has to look like that, to have those features, to have that kind of body. She buys into the myth that her sexuality comes from being "beautiful" rather than understanding that her beauty comes from her sexuality.

And so she tries to attain the unobtainable—to become thinner than nature intended, without realizing that when a woman becomes unnaturally thin, she relinquishes her sexual desires and her love of the most feminine part of her being.

Many women feel ashamed of or threatened by their sexual feelings. It is not uncommon for women who struggle with disordered eating to have had sexual experiences they feel guilty about. They may blame themselves for sexual encounters that were forced upon them as children or chastise themselves for "giving in" to forbidden sexual pleasures as adolescents. They have been taught by traditional religions that if a woman is sensual or sexual, she is bad. Her sexuality is sinful.

Part of the recovery process involves remembering the experiences that disconnected us from the inherent beauty of our sexuality and reclaiming the aspects of our sexuality that were disowned because of those experiences. For one woman it may mean recalling early sexual experiences of masturbation, rubbing up against her cat, or exploring her body with other children, and the shame she felt for responding to her natural sexual instincts so that she can appreciate her innate sensuality. For another, it may mean recounting painful incestuous experiences with her father, brother, uncle, or cousin, or a time when she was caught off guard by the sexual advances of a friend and was not able to say no for fear of hurting his feelings or "making a scene." If a woman feels she cannot say no to unwanted sexual advances, she cannot say yes! to her feminine sexuality. Yet another may recall a period of promiscuity where her focus was on whetting and satisfying the sexual appetites of men in order to feel loved, attractive, and wanted. In order to reclaim her sexuality she must learn to focus on *her* needs, *her* desires and not feel guilty or selfish for wanting to be fulfilled.

Many women who struggle with disordered eating have difficulty experiencing sexual pleasure. Throughout the day, the more they focus on caring for and giving to others, the more they are consumed with food obsessions, the less aware they become of themselves as sexual beings. The practical matters they tend to from day to day take precedence over their deeper sexual nature. They fail to recognize (and therefore are unable to inform their partners) how much they need to be reminded of their sensuality and how much they need a gradual buildup of sexual tension in order to *feel* their sexual desires. And so they focus on sexual performance rather than on receiving sexual pleasure. Sex with their partners becomes just one more task, one more responsibility.

When a woman does not recognize that much of her sexual pleasure can come from the extension of sexual excitement rather than simply the release of sexual tension, she often fails to give herself (or ask for) the time that she needs to let go of the responsibilities of the day and become aroused. She becomes unaware of how much she hungers to feel her desire increase and she mistakenly assumes that her hunger is for food.

If a woman becomes pregnant, any unresolved issues with food, body image, and sexuality can become amplified. If she experienced difficulty honoring her body changes as an adolescent, it may be extremely difficult for her to celebrate the beauty of life growing within her as her body expands. If she felt out of control as her body thrust her into the world of woman before she felt ready, those feelings may resurface as, once again, she finds herself moved by biological forces beyond her command. Her increased appetite and emotional sensitivity can be alarming if she has spent most of her life trying to diminish those aspects of herself. She needs to appreciate that during pregnancy her bodily sensations are most pronounced, providing her with an ideal opportunity to learn her physical hunger signals for when to eat and when to stop eating, to discover subtle signals that can even tell her precisely *what* to eat.

Once in a while, she may catch a glimpse of herself as the embodiment of the sacred Madonna, the Great Earth Mother, but this image is as fleeting as it is quickly overwhelmed by her fear of becoming fat and disfigured, by her revulsion toward her puffy cheeks, disappearing waist, large thighs, and swollen belly. If she knows of no other way to cope with her fears than by focusing on food, fat, and dieting, then this obsession will take over, not allowing her to fully honor and appreciate the wisdom of her body. She becomes unable to see her feminine sexuality as her inherent connection to nature and its most profound expression of power, the power to create life.

A new mother finds little support or recognition in our culture for the concept that feminine sexuality and motherhood are parts of the same whole we call woman. The less pregnant she looks after giving birth, the more people comment on how good she looks. For a woman who has struggled with a poor body image, this can be an extremely difficult time. She cannot fit into her prepregnancy clothes but no longer feels justified in wearing maternity outfits. If she believes that she must be thin in order to be sexual, she may feel unattractive and estranged from her mate.

If her self-esteem and sense of personal power have been based on being thin, she is at risk for becoming depressed. She may feel a sense of urgency to exercise in order to lose weight as quickly as possible, but find that she is too exhausted or too busy with the demands of motherhood. If she has coped with feelings of depression in the past by numbing herself with food, she may enter a vicious cycle of eating to deal with feeling bad about herself and then feeling bad about her eating behavior. If she has a tendency to nourish others endlessly, she will then compensate for feelings of deprivation by eating in an attempt to fulfill her emotional or sexual needs with food.

It is not uncommon for a woman who has felt unfulfilled sexually to try to satisfy herself with certain foods, like chocolate. Eating chocolate becomes the perfect substitute for sex because eating it elicits feelings that are similar to the feelings she may have about her sexuality: it is "sinfully" delicious, it is forbidden, it is sensuous, it is not necessary, she doesn't deserve it, it is bad for her.

A woman who has been cut off from her sexuality hungers for a connection to this deepest part of her feminine nature. She is beset with a longing for wholeness and fulfillment. And because she no longer recognizes what she truly hungers for, she imagines that what she hungers for is food.

To reclaim her true sexual nature, a woman must tune in to her body, her instincts, and her feelings. If we look outside ourselves to define our sexuality, we run the risk of seeing ourselves as sex objects and become vulnerable to feelings of disappointment and self-recrimination for failing to meet the standards of others. When we consider our sexuality as worth exploring from a personal, subjective perspective, we can begin to free ourselves from assumptions about women's sexuality based on patriarchal distortions.

Remember your earliest childhood experiences with sexuality? What kinds of messages were you given by your mother, your father, your brothers or sisters? What kinds of experiences did you have in school when you were entering puberty? What intrigued you? What frightened you? What were the explicit or implicit messages about feminine sexuality you received from your religious upbringing? What experiences have you had that separated you from the true nature of your feminine sexuality? How have you used food to fulfill sexual desires or to distract you from sexual yearnings? How have you used judgments about or obsessions with your body shape to deprive you of the joy of your sexuality?

When we begin to explore our sexuality, we often find that it barely resembles the images we inherited from our culture. Many women discover that the sex act is only one aspect of the totality of their sexuality. Some women discover their sexuality seems to be intimately connected to nature and can be stimulated by a full moon, the scent of a rose, the heat of the sun, or the sound of the ocean. While some women find their sexuality in stillness and silence, other women are aroused by the sound of certain melodies, beats, or rhythms in music. For some women pornographic images can be very exciting, yet other women find them demeaning and a turn-off. While many women may experience their sexuality most profoundly as a desire to feel connected, to communicate with another, others discover that they do not need a partner to experience sexual pleasure or feel sexually fulfilled.

When a woman explores her sexuality, she often discovers that it is cyclical in nature. Instead of a constant, steady, unwavering stream of energy, it seems to ebb and flow like the tides. The times she is most easily aroused may correspond to certain phases of her menstrual cycle, certain times of the day, certain seasons of the year. When you are able to view your sexuality as cyclical, those times when it seems to wane can be experienced as a transition time leading toward renewal, rather than a sign that you are no longer sexual.

To reclaim your true sexual nature, you need to appreciate that we are all entitled to sexual expression. It is part of being human. You do not have to look or act a certain way to deserve to be sexual.

Feeling free to feel sexual desires does not necessarily mean acting them out. Instead of impulsively acting on sexual urges that arise, without any regard for the consequences, you can make conscious choices about how to express your sexuality and can be responsible for your actions. When a woman reconnects with her sexuality as an innate creative life force, she recognizes that it can take many forms as she expands her creative expression of her sexuality to include dance, poetry, art, or music. She understands that embracing her feminine sexuality allows her to have all her senses heightened, be fully present in the moment, to experience her truth, and to feel complete. To be sexual as a woman is to be alive.

15

The Descent

Meeting the Shadow

As a woman in search of freedom from food and weight obsessions makes her way through a labyrinthine tangle of thoughts, feelings, and desires, she eventually comes to a path that plunges her down into the center of her Self. She now realizes that complete recovery requires a willingness to descend deep into the depths of her being, to confront all those aspects of herself that she would just as soon leave hidden in the dark.

In an ancient Sumerian myth, Inanna, the Queen of Heaven and Earth, decided it was time for her to replenish her powers since she was feeling them waning. She knew that in order to do this, she needed to descend into the underworld. Her people pleaded with her not to do this for the underworld was ruled by Inanna's vicious sister, Ereshkigal, Queen of the Great Below. It was a very dangerous place and many of those who journeyed there never returned. Inanna insisted, however, and so her closest assistant devised a plan to send help in the event that Inanna did not return in three days.

Even though Inanna was the Queen of Heaven, Ereshkigal insisted that she enter the underworld the way everyone else had to: by passing through seven gates. At each gateway she had to remove a

*piece of her magnificent regalia and be judged by the gatekeepers. She
arrived in the kingdom of the Great Below, naked and judged by the
seven gatekeepers. Ereshkigal, true to form, killed her and hung her
body on a peg.*

*After three days had passed without Inanna's return, her
assistant set in motion a plan to rescue her. When Inanna's parents
refused to interfere with the ways of the underworld, Inanna's
assistant sought help from Enki, the god of waters and wisdom. Enki
sent two little creatures, neither male nor female, both endowed with
the gift of empathy, to rescue Inanna. The creatures were able to slip
through the gates unnoticed, carrying the food and water of life.*

*When they encountered Ereshkigal, they found her mourning
the recent death of her husband. The two creatures sat with her in her
grief. Ereshkigal was so touched by the empathy they offered and was
so grateful for it (since no one before had ever approached her with
compassion), that she granted them their request for Inanna's body.
They took her body and revived her with the food and water of life
and Inanna returned to her kingdom with her powers fully restored.*

When a woman finds herself frantically wolfing down muffin after muffin, or incapable of chewing a stick of gum without
counting its calories, or unable to stop herself from bingeing or
purging, or seduced into eating the entire cake in the refrigerator,
she feels weak and out of control. Like Inanna, she feels her power
has eroded. And, again like Inanna, she must take the journey
down into the underworld to find a renewed sense of strength.

For the longest time, she has been frightened of this journey
into the darkness, frightened of what horrors she may find there,
and she has dealt with her fear by trying to avoid it, by denying
the importance of the dark places of her being where her deepest
secrets reside. The underworld has continually tried to make its
shadowy presence known and she has persistently tried to keep its

existence out of her awareness: by eating, by watching her weight, by running—anything but confront her shadow sister that lives in the dark and contains all the aspects of herself she has denied, rejected, or repressed. She eventually discovers that whenever we try to disown the shadow parts of our being, they seem to acquire strength and begin to take over our lives in the form of obsessions and addictions. Her eating becomes an addiction, she obsesses about her weight, and finds herself running compulsively.

Exhausted and depleted from her endless struggle for control, she comes to realize that no one can fix her, that there are no miracle pills, no magical diets. At some point she recognizes that the only solution left is to go within, to explore the dark, hidden places of her being and find out why she does what she does with food. She is frightened of being destroyed by some evil aspect of herself that she believes is buried deep within her, hidden from view. In her desperation, she finds the courage to make the descent, to face her fears.

Like Inanna, she discovers that to make the journey, she must shed her clothing, the parts of herself that she shows the outer world, that represent who she thinks she *should* be. And as she begins to reveal to herself the feelings and desires that she has covered up for so long, she encounters all of her self-judgments: "I am too selfish... I am too sensitive... Others won't like who I really am..." and so on. Stripped bare of all the cultural expectations of how she ought to be, she arrives at the center of her being, naked and vulnerable, ready to face the truth about herself.

In meeting Ereshkigal, her shadow sister, she confronts her own dark side, that part of her that has been split off from awareness. As terrifying as it may be to face our shadow sister, to look her in the eye, face her we must because it is she who will reveal the root issues that underlie our distorted relationship with food. She is the keeper of our deepest, darkest secrets. She will tell us about the shame we feel for having suffered, for not being good enough or smart enough or pretty enough—for being sexual, for being different, for being female.

Some women who struggle with disordered eating have deep, shameful secrets that they struggle desperately to keep out of their awareness. One woman may feel so ashamed of her mother's alcoholism that she cannot bear to remember her childhood. Another may suffer deeply from the lack of attention and affection in her upbringing and feel ashamed of her neediness. Yet another may have suffered such physical and emotional abuse that she still feels the sting of her humiliation. But these memories and experiences can never be fully disowned, only relegated to the shadows. And whenever they try to surface up out of the darkness, they come forth in a distorted, toxic form: as food obsessions, secret binges, diets gone out of control.

When a woman chooses, consciously and deliberately, to go into the dark and meet with her shadow sister, she no longer needs to live in fear of her destructive, unannounced visits. As she listens to her shadow sister and honors her suffering, she will not be bombarded with demands for attention.

Because our culture for centuries has banished the true beauty and power of feminine sexuality to the underground, so that it can be discussed only through innuendo and inference, many women with disordered eating have kept secrets about their sexuality they must address. Childhood memories of sexual exploration or teenage memories of promiscuity may need to surface and be recognized and accepted as a natural part of their growth. Their experience of having a woman's body that has been talked about only in hushed tones, laughed at for being fat, or subjected to leering stares, taunting whistles, and sexist ridicule needs to be acknowledged. For one woman, being able to talk about the way her brother's friend "felt her up" and then laughed at her distress was an important part of her recovery process. Another woman was able to stop bingeing and purging only when she revealed that a professor she had held in high esteem had been making unwanted sexual advances. Yet another woman, in order to let go of her obsession with food, needed to tell her story of how she unwillingly lost her virginity to a trusted male friend who had seduced her with alcohol. Many women have had to reveal secret horrors of molestation, rape, and incest so they could be free of the humiliation and self-loathing secret-keeping brings.

When we go to the deepest, darkest part of ourselves, many of us encounter the pain and suffering we have tried to disown. Our patriarchial culture demands that we bear our pain stoically, keep it hidden from view. We have been reprimanded time and time again for engaging in "self-pity" when we have tried to pour out the pain we feel in our hearts. And so we deny our pain and say everything is "all right." As a woman finds the center of herself in this journey toward wholeness, she encounters her deepest pain: the pain of abandonment and isolation, of feeling unworthy and inept, of unrealized dreams and missed opportunities, of physical or emotional abuse, of the loss of loved ones or failed marriages, and the pain that comes with being female in a world that does not honor the feminine.

When a woman who has used food for so long to hide her wounds meets her shadow sister, she is often overwhelmed by the sorrow that permeates this outcast part of her being. She may be flooded with tears and must learn to let them flow, instead of distracting herself prematurely with thoughts of diets, exercise, or food. There is no place in the underworld for coldness toward her own pain, no room for expectations of invulnerability or for denial of her wounds. In the dark, suffering is respected. Pain is allowed.

A woman's descent into herself culminates in death. The old "her" must die in order for rebirth to occur. Her image of herself as victim must die. Her view of herself as wrong, damaged, worthless, unattractive, incompetent must die. Her callous apathy toward her own suffering must die.

In the darkness, she is reborn. Her shadow sister with the power to destroy also holds the power of transformation and renewal. When she meets her, naked and without pretense or denial, she can begin to make sense of her past, perhaps understand what happened and why, discover what lessons are to be learned, what truths she needs to realize. She can receive the inner wisdom that will enable her to create a whole new way of being with food, with others, and with herself.

In the end, it is empathy, the ability to view herself, her feelings, and her needs with understanding and appreciation, that comes to the rescue. It is the ability to "be with" her pain that helps her move through it slowly so that deep healing can occur. Because of this empathy, she is able to discern the connections between her upbringing and her disordered eating without blaming herself or others for her situation, and without denying her wounds.

When Ereshkigal feels heard, she allows the creatures to restore Inanna to life and nourish her with the food and water of life. Only when her shadow sister is heard with compassion and understanding can a woman receive the real nourishment she desires in her own life.

In order to heal her disordered eating, a woman must embrace the darkness that precedes renewal. She must recover the rejected and lost parts of herself, retrieve her disowned experiences and denied feelings, and integrate them into the wholeness of her being. It is this wholeness that strengthens a woman and holds the promise of renewal and change.

16

Assertiveness

Speaking the Truth

There was once a young knight who had committed the most horrible crime a man could commit against a woman. For this crime he was arrested and brought before the king for sentencing. The king said, "This crime is so terrible that I think it is only fair to let the woman you have wronged decide your sentence." He called the woman forth and asked her what the young man's punishment should be. She said, "He should be given a riddle to solve, and if he does not solve this riddle within one year's time, he should be put to death."

The king said, "And what is the riddle?"

She said, "The riddle is this. He is to answer the question "What is it that a woman desires most?"'

The king turned to the young man and said, "So be it. You are to return exactly one year from today with the answer to this riddle. If you do not have the correct answer, you will be put to death."

Well, the young knight walked out through the courtyard pleased to have been let off so easily, with only a silly question to answer. He hadn't gotten very far when he saw a beautiful young woman coming his way. With a big smile on his face, he approached her and said, "Excuse me, Miss, can you please tell me what is it that a woman desires most?"

She cocked her head, looked at him coyly and said, "A lover. A lover is what a woman desires most."

The young man thanked her and began to head on his way when he spotted a middle-aged woman walking down the road with a babe in arms and four small children tugging on her skirts. He walked up to her and said, "Excuse me, Ma'am, would you mind telling me what is it that a woman desires most?"

"Peace!" she exclaimed. "Peace is what a woman desires most."

He thanked her and headed on his way.

Within a short while he came across an old lady hobbling along with a cane. He went up to her and politely said, "Excuse me, Ma'am, would you mind telling me what is it that a woman desires most?"

"That's easy," she said without hesitation. "Health is what a woman desires most."

He thanked her, but as he continued on his way, he grew concerned. "I've asked three different women the answer to this riddle," he thought, "and I've gotten three different answers. This might not be as easy as I'd first thought." So he went and got a book with blank pages and wrote the answers down.

The young man then proceeded to travel through many villages, towns, and into the countryside, offering the riddle to each woman he encountered and writing down her response in his book. The days turned into weeks, the weeks turned into months, and the months turned into . . . well, it was not quite a year when the young man found himself sitting on a curb with his head in his hands.

"In one more day, an entire year will have passed," he sobbed in despair. "I have asked thousands of women this question and have received thousands of different answers. I am no closer to solving the riddle than I was when I first heard it. Tomorrow I will be a dead man!"

Just then, he heard a voice close by. "Excuse me, may I help you?"

He looked up and there, in front of him, stood the ugliest creature he had ever seen! Her head was too big for her body. Her eyes were too big for her head. She had a long, pointy nose, thin lips, and teeth like splinters. Her hair hung down to her shoulders like rat tails, and she had skin like the belly of a dead fish.

"Why are you crying?" she asked.

"Well," said the young man, "I have been given a riddle to solve, and if I don't solve it by tomorrow I shall lose my life."

"What is the riddle?" she asked.

"I am to find the answer to the question 'What is it a woman desires most?'" he replied.

"Oh, I know the answer to that riddle," she said, "and I would be happy to tell it to you if you would agree to marry me."

The young man was taken aback by this woman's request, but thought, "What does it matter? Without the answer to this riddle, I am a dead man. Better I live with this ugly shrew than lose my life." So he agreed to marry her and, in that moment, waited for her response.

The woman spoke, "The answer to the riddle is this. What a woman desires most is sovereignty, the right to create her own path through life."

The knight thought about this and of all the other answers he'd been given. "Yes!" he exclaimed. "This fits with all that I have been told. It is the correct answer!"

And so, in a flurry of excitement, he headed off to the town where he had received his sentence just one year before. The next day he found himself facing the king and the woman he had wronged.

"Well," said the king, "do you have the answer to the riddle?"

"Yes, I do, sire," the young man replied.

"What is it?" demanded the king.

"The answer to the riddle 'What is it that a woman desires most?' is 'Sovereignty, the right to create her own path through life.'"

The king turned to the woman standing beside him and asked, "Is that correct?"

"Yes, it is, your honor," she replied.

"Well, then," said the king, "you are a free man. Be on your way."

This time the young knight nearly flew through the courtyard, filled with relief and a sense of newfound freedom. But, true to his word, he returned to the place where he had met the ugly woman, intent on keeping his side of their bargain. As he had promised, they went to be married, and after their wedding, they journeyed to a small inn where they'd planned to spend their first night together. Upon arriving at the inn, the ugly woman went upstairs to the bridal suite, while the young man went immediately into the tavern.

Hours passed, and eventually the tavern keeper told the young man that he must leave, as he was closing for the night. And so, very slowly, the young man grudgingly climbed the narrow staircase to the room where he knew his bride was waiting.

He reached the room, slowly opened the door, and peered inside. There, across the room, he saw a large bed upon which lay his bride, her hair soiling the pillows. Gingerly, he made his way across the room.

"Husband, come," she said as she patted the bed.

The young knight sat on the very edge of the bed and, ever so slowly, first removed one boot, then the other. He took off his trousers and shirt, and then, completely naked, he slid between the bedsheets. He lay next to her, stiff as a board, with his arms pressed tight against his sides and his face riveted straight ahead.

"Husband, it is our wedding night. Kiss me," she implored.

And so, scrunching up his face, he pursed his lips, closed his eyes tightly, and kissed her. But, as he kissed her, his lips brushed against her cheek, and he was startled because it did not feel like the belly of a dead fish. He opened his eyes and was amazed to be face to face with the most beautiful woman he had ever seen!

"Who are you and what are you doing here?" he blurted out, as soon as he could speak.

"I am your wife," she said. "I was under a spell and when you agreed to marry me and kissed me, you broke the spell. Well," she clarified, "you have broken part of the spell. Now it needs to be decided if I am to be beautiful by day and ugly by night or beautiful by night and ugly by day."

"That's easy," the young man responded quickly, "beautiful by day and ugly by night."

"Well," she said, "that means that every night when you come to lie with me I will be ugly."

"Oh," the young man said as he sucked his breath between his teeth and shuddered at the thought. "Then, ugly by day and beautiful by night."

"Then that means that whenever we walk down the road together, people will shrink away in horror at my ugliness and children will throw stones and taunt me."

"That's not good, either," said the young man as he shook his head, contemplating this new puzzle. After thinking for a moment, he said, "You know, it doesn't seem quite right for me to make this decision. After all, it is you that will have to live with the consequences."

"Ah," said the now beautiful woman, "you have just broken the second half of the spell. For what a woman desires most is sovereignty, the right to create her own path through life. And, since it is my choice, I choose to be beautiful by day and beautiful by night!"

For a woman to create her own path through life she needs to be able to make her own choices, to say yes to what she wants and no to what she doesn't want. Without such freedom to choose, she can become quite "ugly" toward others: sullen and resentful over being taken advantage of, or full of rage and accusatory when she gives to others more than she receives in return.

Achieving this kind of sovereignty is essential to the well-being of all women but it is especially important to the woman struggling with food, fat, and dieting. This woman is cast under a spell of helplessness and hopelessness, a spell that must be broken. In order to be freed from this spell she needs to learn how to assert her inherent rights to choose what she desires and to reject what is not right for her.

Assertiveness is an essential tool for achieving sovereignty in one's life. In becoming assertive, a woman finds a way to express who she is and what she wants. She learns how to communicate without being passive and neglectful of her needs or being aggressive and insensitive to the needs of others.

When a woman communicates passively, she says yes to things when she wants to say no, and no to things when she wants to say yes. She acts as though things are okay when they are not. Because of this, the path she takes through life is not her own, and she cannot receive the gifts that come through living her own destiny. Her choices are guided not by what she feels and wants for herself but by the needs and desires of others. Her spirit becomes impoverished and her sense of her authentic self, who she really is, gets weakened. Lacking a connection with this deeper self, she is in touch with only her outer shell, the most superficial aspect of who she is. She does not know her true self and does not show it to the outside world. Instead, she becomes overly focused on her appearance, on how she looks to others. She strives to appear "nice," sweet, accommodating, and pleasant at all times at the expense of her sense of self: her self-esteem, her self-direction, and her self-confidence.

Not wanting to risk displeasing others, she is quick to respond with comments such as "Oh, it's no big deal," "It really doesn't matter," "I don't care," "You decide." Eventually she begins to believe that how she thinks and feels really *doesn't* matter, that who she is really doesn't matter. Not only does she convince herself that this is so, she manages to convince those around her that her thoughts and feelings have no value. When she diminishes her self-worth in this way, others are quick to follow suit. And when others begin to disregard her needs and treat her poorly, her tolerance of their mistreatment encourages this behavior to continue. Finding herself on a path through life that drains, rather than nourishes her, she turns to food for relief, for sustenance, or solace. Eating becomes a vain attempt to feed her depleted self-esteem. Believing that she doesn't deserve nourishment because she has failed to please those around her, she may deprive herself of food or reprimand herself for eating when she truly is hungry. And her life becomes emptier than ever.

On the other hand, the woman who is aggressive, rather than passive, and ferverently defends her sovereignty by attacking others, may get some of the things she wants in life, but she is constantly having to confront the fallout of her accusatory words and harsh actions. In an attempt to express her true feelings, she lashes out at others, only to end up feeling misunderstood and alone. Her journey through life becomes a trail of broken relationships. She feels the sting of the rejection her "ugliness" brings.

Unable to comprehend any other way of taking care of herself, she believes she has only two choices: ugly by day or ugly by night. She knows how to get what she wants and needs but doesn't know how to do it without disregarding the needs and feelings of others. In the end, unable to find the nourishment that close relationships might bring her, she turns to food for comfort and companionship.

Many women find themselves swinging like pendulums between passivity and aggressiveness. They are passive, passive, passive until they can no longer contain their feelings, and then suddenly they swing over and become aggressive, hurling insults and accusatory remarks at whoever angers or threatens them. Then guilt sets in and the cycle starts all over again.

Some of these women find themselves using food to stuff down their angry feelings. Others may find themselves bingeing and purging in an attempt to alternately shove down their feelings and then gain relief by unleashing the built-up tension that comes with holding back feelings.

If a woman wants to obtain true sovereignty, she must learn to protect her rights in a way that honors the rights of others. She must learn to be assertive: to stand up for herself, to express her feelings, and to state what she wants without blaming, without threats and accusations. She must treat her own thoughts and feelings with respect while respecting the thoughts and feelings of others. That is the only way she is going to be able to feel good about herself and have the kinds of relationships she desires.

To get a picture of how this is done, imagine that a friend borrowed a book from you. You told her at the time that she was free to read the book as long as she returned it the following Friday because you needed it for a report you were working on. However, for one reason or another, she failed to return the book. You were able to complete your report but not without some difficulty.

One week later you run into her at the supermarket and she suddenly remembers the book you had loaned her. She apologizes for not returning it on time. If you were to respond passively, you might say something like "Oh, it's okay. It's no big deal," when the truth is that you felt inconvenienced by her behavior and even somewhat resentful.

Although your intent in not expressing your true feelings might have been to avoid upsetting your friend, tension builds up within you and between the two of you because you are feeling anger that you don't want her to know about. She may sense the tension but not know why you seem cool or distant. And the next time she borrows something the same thing might happen again, because you have already given her the impression that these things don't matter to you. After a few more incidents like this, the tension might build up to the point where you decide to pull away from the relationship, and not even tell her why.

If you were, instead, to respond to this situation aggressively, you might react to your friend with accusations such as "I can't believe you did that! How can you be so inconsiderate? Didn't I tell you I needed that book back by Friday? Thanks a lot!"

Although in this scenario you are expressing your feelings about being inconvenienced, you are doing it in a way that is hurtful. You are calling her names ("inconsiderate"), and using an accusatory tone that implies something is wrong with her. As a result, your friend will feel attacked and to protect herself may decide to pull away from you, maybe even terminate the relationship altogether.

An assertive approach to this situation would be very different from either of those scenarios. It would include expressing your feelings but doing it in a way that involved neither attacking nor blaming. For example, after your friend's apology, you might say something like "Well, it was frustrating not having that book for my report. The next time you borrow something, please return it on time."

Although you have let her know that what she did was not okay with you, you didn't attack who she is as a person. She may feel bad about her behavior, but not because you put her down. Since you expressed your feelings honestly, your resentment toward her can pass. Rather than creating distance or tension between the two of you, you have expressed your desire for the relationship to continue, implying that you expect to loan her things in the future. She is not left having to second-guess your feelings, to figure out where she stands in the relationship. And you are not left with guilt, loneliness, or the tension of feelings left unexpressed.

In my experience working with women struggling with disordered eating, I've not seen anyone recover without first learning to be assertive. It is probably the most important skill needed because it is the means by which we embrace and express the essence of who we really are without being destructive to others. It is how we ensure that we are on the right path, the path of the heart, that leads us to people and places that are nourishing and fulfilling and steers us away from those that are not.

Like any other skill, however, it takes practice and a willingness to go through a certain clumsy phase before achieving mastery. This is not unlike the experience of learning to ride a bicycle as a child. Remember how overwhelming it was to try to pedal, to keep your balance, to steady the handle bars, and to watch where you were going all at the same time? This is the kind of awkwardness you might expect as you learn to be assertive. Eventually, though, with a little practice, this way of communicating can begin to feel as effortless and natural as riding a bicycle.

There are three assertiveness techniques I recommend learning. The first is a basic formula for expressing yourself. Because it can sometimes be difficult to think clearly in the "heat of the moment," the simplicity of this formula can be really helpful. You have to remember only five words:

When you . . .
I feel . . .
Because . . .

For the first part, fill in the blank with a description of the behavior that triggered your feelings:

When you talk to me like that . . .
When you look at me that way . . .
When you say . . .
When you borrow my book and don't return it . . .

Describe the behavior as specifically and as objectively as possible, being careful not to make any assumptions about the other person's intent, such as "When you put me down like that . . ." or "When you act like you know what's best for me . . . ."

For the second part, take a moment to check in and see how you are feeling, and then state the feeling as clearly as you can.

I feel angry . . .
I feel frustrated . . .
I feel hurt . . .
I feel confused . . .

Try to narrow it down to one or two feelings so you can remain focused. It is important that you take responsibility for your feelings and not say, "You make me feel . . . ," because the other person will feel that you are blaming or attacking them. Rather than listening to what you are saying, they will be busy preparing a defense or counterattack and the doors to communication will close.

For the third part, ask yourself, "Why does this behavior trigger these feelings? How do I interpret what they are doing?" For example:

Because it gives me the impression you don't care about me . . .
Because I get the idea you don't trust me . . .
Because it seems like you think you know better than I do what's best for me . . .
Because I get the impression you were putting me down . . .

When being assertive, it's best to keep it short. With this formula, you can say what you need to say in just one sentence. You don't want to get lost in a lot of words but rather get right to the point.

It's important to understand that it is not necessary to be assertive in the moment that the behavior occurs. In fact, while you are learning to be assertive, more often than not you won't be able to think on your feet. That's fine. There's absolutely nothing wrong with using the formula in the past tense:

"Last month when you canceled our lunch date, I felt hurt, because it gave me the impression that getting together with me wasn't very important to you."

"Yesterday, when you yelled at me to hurry up, I felt angry because it seemed to me that you were blaming me for being late."

"I didn't realize it at the time, but last week when you suggested that I quit my job, I felt angry because I thought you were criticizing me for not spending more time with my son."

Often people struggling with disordered eating dream of a magical solution or some instant resolution. While this rarely occurs, these five words (when you . . . I feel . . . because) can truly be magical when used with consistency. While you are learning to be assertive, you may find it helpful to write them on a card that you can carry with you or keep next to your telephone.

When you first begin to use the formula, you might want to explain to others with whom you have important relationships why you are letting them know how their behavior is affecting your feelings so they don't interpret this change in your behavior as simply your "picking" on them. For example, you might say something like "The reason I want to talk to you about this is that I know I have a tendency to pull away when something upsets me. Our relationship means so much to me, though, that I don't want to jeopardize it by withdrawing." Or: "When I don't let you know you're doing something that's not okay with me, I become so resentful and grouchy it hurts our relationship. I don't want to keep doing something that is so hurtful."

The second assertiveness technique I recommend learning is one that builds on the first. Sometimes when a woman uses "the formula" and asserts her feelings, others respond aggressively, by attacking her or by blaming her for creating conflict. This technique for responding to aggressive behavior is called "deflection" because it helps to turn away verbal attacks, accusations, and put-downs. It is a way of sidestepping destructive arguments over who's right and who's wrong, which usually lead nowhere.

When someone tells you "You're just too sensitive," or "It's stupid to feel that way," or, simply, "You're wrong," it's important that you not act as though you have to defend yourself. Instead, sidestep the accusation with a comment like

"That may be so . . ." (You are neither agreeing nor disagreeing with them.)
    "I realize that is your perspective . . ."
    "I can appreciate your point of view . . ."

and then follow up with your perception:

". . . But that is how I feel."
". . . But I see things differently."
". . . But I want you to know how your behavior affects me."

When you use this technique, you will be amazed at how easily you can stay focused on how you feel, what you want and don't want. You will feel the strength that comes from within (the power of dominion) when you honor your feelings as well as those of others. You are asserting that you *can* have a difference in perspective without having to end the relationship or abandon your thoughts and feelings.

The third technique is one that follows deflection and is called the "broken record" because it involves repeating yourself over and over when you are communicating your feelings and the other person responds with an attack. For example, let's say you told your husband that when he said, "Are you sure you want to eat that?" you felt angry because it gave you the impression he thought he knew better than you what you should and shouldn't eat. He responded by saying, "Well, you're obviously not doing too good a job handling your food."

Instead of getting sidetracked with the issue of how well you are handling your disordered eating, your first response could be to "deflect" by saying, "That may be so," and then to restate your feelings, "But I want you to know that when you tell me what I should or shouldn't eat, I feel angry."

If he says something like "Gee, aren't we being a little touchy?" you "deflect" by saying, "Maybe," and then, "But I want you to know when you tell me what I should or shouldn't eat, I feel angry." He might say, "I think you are really overreacting," and you can respond once again with, "It may seem that way to you, but I want you to know that when you tell me what to eat or not to eat, I get angry."

If he stays with the argument and says, "Well, if you could get it together better, I wouldn't have to say anything," you can continue with the broken record, "It's important to me that you know that when you tell me what to eat or not to eat, I feel angry." Notice that you are not telling him what he should or should not be doing, not attacking him, but simply letting him know how his behavior affects you.

When you are using the broken record, you remain focused on your feelings and keep yourself from getting distracted by other issues and accusations. Perhaps not in that moment, but eventually, the other person will stop mudslinging and maybe even hear what you have to say. In any case, you are still taking care of yourself by identifying and expressing your feelings.

One of the first reactions I get when someone is learning to be assertive is "It won't work," "She won't listen to me," "He won't stop what he is doing." It is important to know that if your goal for being assertive is to get the other person to change, to be different, chances are you're going to be very frustrated. If, however, your goal for being assertive is to feel better about yourself, then your odds for success increase.

Assertiveness is probably the most important skill a woman must learn to begin to break free from disordered eating. Once she recognizes that she is eating or not eating in response to emotional stress rather than physical hunger, she is faced with the task of responding to that stress in another way. The reason diets don't work is that they focus on removing the disordered eating behavior without replacing it with another way to address the feelings and the underlying issues that trigger the behavior in the first place.

As a woman becomes assertive, she develops a new, much more effective way of dealing with the stresses life can bring. She discovers that assertiveness can have a profound effect on her relationship with food and eating. By learning to ask for what she wants, she learns to identify, seek out, and feed her emotional hungers in appropriate ways so that she becomes less likely to turn to food for nourishment.

As she learns to say no to what she doesn't want, she defines her personal boundaries. By saying to others, "My needs are different, not more or less important than yours," she establishes where she begins and ends and where others begin and end. This allows her to feel secure in her ability to set limits and therefore more comfortable with intimacy. She no longer needs to fear losing herself or being swallowed up in her relationships. And the more closeness she allows herself, the less she feels compelled to soothe her loneliness with food.

When a woman becomes assertive, she develops the skills she needs to deal with disagreements in her relationships and no longer needs to do whatever she is doing with food to avoid conflict. She is able to sidestep the blaming, accusatory behavior that interferes with the discussion of the real issues and the resolution of the conflicts. She discovers there is room to agree to disagree.

When she expresses her thoughts and feelings openly and directly, her self-esteem and self-confidence increase because she is affirming that her thoughts and feelings matter, that who she is matters. Her tendency to starve herself or overeat whenever she feels bad about herself decreases as her sense of self-worth increases.

Speaking her truth becomes a way of life. She no longer has to use food to fend off the nagging anxiety that comes with acting one way when feeling another or to fill the pit in her stomach she gets from saying yes when she wanted to say no.

Many women who struggle with disordered eating believe that when they are thinner, they will magically solve the riddle of their unhappiness. They cling to this belief even when they look at old pictures of themselves at the weight they would like to be at now and remember how unhappy (and fat) they felt then. They don't yet understand that happiness is a state of mind (not body). It is not a goal they can set the way they establish their ideal weight. It is a by-product of being in their own truth, choosing their own path through life. When these women grow more assertive, they become happier, and as they become happier they no longer need to use food to numb out tension and misery. Their bodies then become free to find the weights that are right for them.

When a woman becomes increasingly skilled at being assertive, she finds herself feeling more and more in control of her life. She realizes that although she may not be able to control her feelings, she can control how she expresses them. She no longer has to worry about losing control and wreaking havoc in others' lives. Free from the incredible pressure that comes from trying to do the impossible (control her feelings), she no longer needs to be obsessed with controlling her weight or food intake in order to give herself the illusion of being in control.

An assertive woman is one who honors the most feminine aspects of her being. She is able to create a vessel strong enough to contain the power of her feminine spirit, her deepest truths and her strongest emotions, and can use her masculine energy to take it out into the world. She is able to address and communicate that which is invisible, those matters of the heart that we are so often moved by but find so hard to describe and validate. She is at home in this invisible world. no longer haunted by a deep-seated belief that something is wrong with her because she feels things so strongly, because she is so responsive to things that cannot be validated by her five senses. When she is able to describe the behavior that triggers her feelings, she can open the gateway to understanding and accepting her feelings, to truly understanding and accepting her feminine nature.

An assertive woman can have an impact on our patriarchial society's concept of power and control, which polarizes the possible positions one can take when dealing with power: aggressive or passive, bully or victim, winner or loser. She refuses to be restricted by an either . . . or construct (either I am right or you are) and suggests, instead, the possibility of a yes . . . and construct (yes, you feel that way and I feel this way). She moves beyond the domination dynamics of power-over-others and embraces the beauty of dominion, the power-from-within. She demonstrates how it is possible to hold one's power and stand side by side with another, without one diminishing the power of the other.

An assertive woman claims her sovereignty, her right to create her own path through life. In this way she can choose to be beautiful by day and beautiful by night.

17

Nourishment

Physical versus Emotional

This old tale from China is about a magic pear tree:

Once, a long, long time ago, a prosperous farmer brought his pears to the marketplace. This was a fine year for pears, and his pears were so plump, sweet, and juicy that many in the marketplace gathered around his wagon to buy them. As he stood in the midst of the crowd, beaming with pride over his successful harvest, a woman wearing coarse clothing and tattered scarves approached the farmer and begged for some fruit. The farmer tried to shoo her away, yelling and cursing at her, but the woman would not budge.

"You have so many pears in your cart," she said, "and I would like just one. Surely it would be no great loss to you."

Some in the crowd tried to convince the farmer to part with one of his pears. Others began to yell and shout at the woman and a great commotion ensued. A market guard, concerned that the uproar would get out of hand, tossed the woman a few coins to purchase a piece of fruit.

The woman thanked the guard and said to crowd, "It is difficult to understand such greed for material things. Let me offer you kind customers some fruit."

"You have your pear, now," someone replied. "Why don't you eat it yourself?"

"All I needed was one seed," said the woman as she proceeded to gobble up the pear. She then reached under her garments, pulled out a small shovel, and began to dig a hole in the earth. She placed a seed from the pear in the ground and covered it with dirt. She asked for a little water and a bystander fetched some from a shop nearby. As she poured the water over the newly planted seed, all eyes were upon these strange proceedings.

To their astonishment, a tiny shoot appeared out of the ground. It grew steadily until it became a full-grown tree, with a canopy of green leaves. In an instant it burst into bloom and then was laden with luscious fruit. The woman picked the pears and passed them out to the onlookers who were entranced by this spectacle. When the fruit was all gone, the woman began to chop down the tree with her shovel, hacking away until the tree fell. And then hoisting the upper part of the tree upon her shoulders, she sauntered away.

The farmer, meanwhile, had forgotten his business and stood there with his mouth gaping. But after the woman had departed and he returned to his wagon, he noticed that all his pears were gone! "It was my *pears she distributed!" he exclaimed as he inspected the pears she had presented to the crowd. He then noticed that the handle of his wagon had been chopped off. After much searching, he found it discarded in the corner of the marketplace. He now realized that he had been tricked and the pear tree he had seen cut down was in fact the handle to his wagon.*

Laughter filled the marketplace. The farmer was enraged with his own foolishness. And the tattered woman was never to be seen again.

A woman who desires to be freed from her struggles with disordered eating must develop an ability to see through the illusion that only food can give her sustenance. Until she is able to distinguish physical hunger from symbolic hunger, she remains vulnerable to deception, like the farmer in the story.

Without the ability to recognize the difference between these two hungers, she will desperately cling to food or calorie counting and be unwilling to release her disordered eating patterns. Like the farmer who had a full wagon but an empty heart, she will continue to feel as though she doesn't have enough to spare, that she can't afford to let go of what she is doing with food.

Our minds can play all kinds of tricks on us, but out bodies never lie. If we are listening only to the promptings of our minds and not listening to the messages from our bodies, we can be easily tricked into thinking that we are hungry for food when it is something else we desire. And so we eat and we eat. Before we know it, the plate is empty, the pot scraped clean, and we are left feeling dissatisfied and angry at ourselves for having been so foolish.

The ability to distinguish between physical hunger and emotional hunger is an essential skill that someone struggling with disordered eating needs to develop.

Imagine that within us we all have two containers that we carry on our journey through life. One is a gourd-shaped vessel for carrying food and water, and the other is a heart-shaped basket for carrying all the things we need to make our life meaningful and fulfilling. The gourd is what we fill when we need physical nourishment. It is to be filled with food. The basket is what we fill when we need emotional nourishment. It is to be filled with attention, affection, appreciation and other "foods" for the heart and soul.

A woman with disordered eating patterns fails to distinguish one container from the other. When she she feels hungry, she begins to eat. Before she knows it, her gourd is bursting at the seams. But she finds herself still feeling hungry. She does not realize that even though the gourd is full, her heart basket is empty and needs to be filled. She must learn to distinguish one kind of hunger from the other.

There are really two different kinds of hungers, those that come from the stomach and those that come from the heart. The hunger of the stomach must satisfied with food, but the hunger of the heart must be satisfied with love, with emotional nourishment. Once a woman learns how to recognize the difference between her physical stomach-hunger and her emotional heart-hunger, her needs for food and her longings for emotional sustenance, and how to respond to them, she no longer has to worry about becoming fat.

Like animals in the wild, we all have a built-in gift from Mother Nature that tells us when to eat and when to stop eating, when to drink and when to stop drinking. In their natural habitat, there are no fat zebras, cheetahs, or giraffes. Even hippopotami are just the size they were meant to be. Left to their own devices, these animals grow into the size that is right for them. They eat in response to the internal, instinctive signals they receive from their bodies. They eat when they are hungry for food and stop when they are full.

Some domesticated animals, however, can become overweight because Mother Nature's messages have been preempted by the messages from our culture. They learn, just as we have, to respond to external rather than internal cues. They eat because it's "dinnertime," because others are eating, because it tastes good, because food is a reward for being "good," or because they have learned that being fed means they are loved.

Like all animals in nature, we are born with the ability to know when we are physically hungry. As young babies, we cried and demanded to be fed, not according to the clock or our parents' schedules but according to when our bodies needed to be nourished. A feeling of emptiness in the stomach let us know that it was time to eat. But this pristine and simple process became increasingly complicated as we were expected to accommodate the needs of others, first our families, then the larger culture. We were taught to stop listening to our internal signals, to disregard our inner authority, and, instead, to pay attention to external cues. We might have been instructed to eat with our families whether we were hungry or not. We might have been punished for not eating what was on our plate, even if someone else had decided what and how much to put on it. We might have been prodded to eat when we weren't hungry in order to be free from guilt over "the poor children starving in China." We might have eagerly become members of the "clean plate club" so we could get some dessert.

Eventually we stopped listening to the quiet, soft whispers of our bodies, and were left able to recognize only the more blaring messages like "I'm famished!" or "I'm stuffed!" We forgot about our gift from Mother Nature and became caught up in the illusion that our bodies can't be trusted and must be either ignored or controlled. We lost trust in our own true nature.

The path to recovery from disordered eating inevitably leads us back to a place of attunement with our bodies, a place where the wisdom of our bodies is honored and our trust in them restored. To get there we first must learn how to listen.

I have found a couple of body awareness exercises to be helpful for getting back in touch with those physical sensations that tell us when to eat and drink, and when to stop eating and drinking. Thirst, like a need for food, is a kind of physical hunger, but I have found that the signals for thirst are less likely to get entangled with heart hungers and, for that reason, are easier to begin with. For these exercises, I suggest you drink only water and drink only when you are thirsty.

Next time you begin to feel thirsty, ask yourself, "How do I know that I am thirsty? What is the physical signal that is telling me I am thirsty?" You might be able to recognize a signal such as a dry throat, a dry tongue, or some other physical sensation.

Then ask yourself, "Okay, how do I know when to stop drinking once I have started?" This answer may not come as quickly, but it is important to understand that there is a very specific physical sensation in our bodies that tells us when to stop drinking. This sensation can be different for different people. For one person it may be as soon as her mouth no longer feels dry; for another, it may come when she feels a certain coolness in her throat. What is important is that you recognize what your particular signal is. Keep paying attention in this way until you are certain of your physical thirst signals, those that tell you that you need to drink, as well as those that tell you when it is time to stop.

For most of us, the signals of thirst and quenched thirst are identified much more easily than hunger and fullness signals because we have received less pressure to ignore those messages. But the same basic exercise can be applied to help you rediscover you food-hunger signals.

Ask yourself, "How do I know when I am hungry? What is the physical sensation that tells me I am hungry?" It is not unusual for some women to respond, "I feel light headed and dizzy," or "My stomach starts growling loudly." That is not the signal for hunger, that is the signal for famished! The signal for hunger is much more subtle. It is important to recognize the difference between feeling hungry and feeling famished because if you wait to eat until you are famished, the chances of your overeating are great. You will then say to yourself, "See, I can't trust myself to eat when I am hungry!" and begin to feel very discouraged and out of control. You will most likely not allow yourself to eat again until you can't stand it any longer (because you are famished), and then you will once again overeat, setting up a vicious cycle of discouragement.

The physical sensation for hunger is different for different people. Some people identify it as a tightness in their upper torso, others as a hollowness in their belly, still others as a tension in their chest. It is important to recognize your personal signal, not to look for someone else's. With practice it will become a very clear, unmistakable signal that you will recognize in its most subtle form.

The second part of this task is to identify what fullness feels like to you. Once again ask yourself, "What is the physical signal that tells me when to stop eating?" Many women are stunned by this question because it has been so long since they listened for this signal that they don't believe it exists. They need to be reassured that we all have a fullness signal, but for many of us it is buried beneath a whole pile of other messages such as, "I should stop eating when my plate is empty." Some women can only identify the sensations that comes after fullness: "When I can't eat another bite," or "When I can't move." This is not full. This is stuffed. The signal for being full is much more subtle but with practice will become unmistakable. In fact, you may eventually learn to recognize not just the physical sensation that tells you that you are full but the physical sensation that comes just before it, the one that tells you, "One more bite and I will be full."

Apply the same exercise for learning to recognize your thirst to learning to recognize your hunger. Whenever you reach for something to eat, ask yourself, "What is the physical sensation that is telling me I am hungry? Where in my body do I feel it?" If you can only recognize the sensation for famished, that's okay. Start with that. Take a few bites then ask yourself, "Am I still hungry?" If the answer is "Yes," ask yourself, "How do I know? What is the physical signal?" You may no longer feel famished but you'll recognize that you are still hungry. Look for the specific physical sensation that is telling you that you are hungry. Locate it in your body. Take a few bites and then see if it is still there. Keep taking a few bites at a time, continually asking yourself, "Am I still hungry?" (identifying your physical signal every step of the way) until the answer is "No." Then look for the specific physical sensation that is telling you that you are full and locate it in your body.

It is important to identify your signals as specifically as possible (not something vague, like "I just feel hungry" or "I feel empty" or "I feel satisfied") and locate where in your body you experience them. You need to be able to describe them in physical terms. Do you feel a warmth or a coolness? A smoothness or roughness? An expansion or contraction? A movement or stillness? A heaviness or lightness? A loosening or tightening?

Imagine that you have just met an extraterrestrial who has come to our planet for a couple of weeks to promote world peace and needs to learn to eat and drink in order to survive. This E.T. is asking you, "How do I know when to eat and drink? What does it feel like? How do I know when to stop?" What would you tell her? What specific physical sensations would you describe?

A woman beginning her journey toward recovery from disordered eating may feel discouraged when she is unable to recognize her physical signals right away. She may begin to feel like there is something wrong with her or that she is failing. That is why it is important to remember that finding those signals can take weeks of concentrated focus and attention. She needs to be reminded that while she may at first be able to identify only the very loud and dramatic signals of "famished" and "stuffed," in time she will develop a more refined power of discernment. More subtle signals will reveal themselves to her.

And the power and depth of that discernment will be extraordinary.

Without diet books, calorie counters, fat charts and the like, she will find that the inner wisdom of her body will guide her toward those choices that are most truly nourishing and healthy. She will be astonished to discover that her internal "computer" provides her with far more accurate information about her needs and desires than any other external source might provide. She'll learn that her body itself will assess not only how many grams of fat she's consumed or calories burned, but that it will also take into account her metabolic rate, the amount of sleep or exercise she gets, where she is in her menstrual cycle, the amount of stress she has been experiencing and much, much more. She will discover that she does not have to do any fancy calculations or analysis: all she needs to do is get to know and trust her body.

As she learns to trust her body signals, she discovers that if she eats when she is *physically* hungry and stops when she is full, she can eat what she wants and not get fat. The only criterion she needs for eating is physical hunger. She no longer needs to worry about fattening foods versus dietetic foods, good foods versus bad foods. If she eats something high in fat, her body knows it takes longer to digest fatty foods and will not signal her to eat until much later than usual. As she allows her body to be her guide, in time she will find that it will steer her toward those foods that are more nutritious, that make her cells sing. Her body will only want what it really needs, not what other people say is good for her.

Understanding how different foods affect her body can be helpful for a woman who is trying to eat in response to her physical appetite. Most of us do not have work or school schedules that allow us the flexibility to eat at any moment we feel hungry. We need to know a little about how our body processes the foods we eat so that we can use food to accommodate our busy lifestyles rather than centering our lives around food and eating.

If, for example, a woman decides to have a jelly doughnut for breakfast, her blood sugar is going to rise very quickly and then drop dramatically shortly thereafter. The simple sugars found in the jelly doughnut are digested by her body very rapidly, and she will find herself feeling hungry again within a fairly short period of time. If instead of a jelly doughnut, she has a piece of whole wheat toast with some jelly on it, her body will respond differently. Although her blood sugar will rise quickly because of the simple sugars in the jelly, it will drop more gradually because the complex carbohydrates in the bread take longer to digest, and it will take longer for her to feel hungry again. If she adds some peanut butter to the toast, she will get yet another response from her body. The simple sugar in the jelly will bring her immediate relief from her hunger, but the fat and protein in the peanut butter will be digested even more slowly than the carbohydrates in the bread, lengthening the amount of time until she is hungry even further.

As we pay more attention to what we eat in terms of how long it takes us to digest certain foods, we can plan our meals accordingly. If you are hungry but plan to go out to dinner in a couple of hours, you might choose to eat something that will satisfy your hunger (like an apple) but not something that will take awhile to digest (like a cheese sandwich). If you are not hungry at breakfast time but know you will be famished before lunch, take something with you to snack on later (a piece of fruit, trail mix, crackers) that you have discovered will carry you until lunchtime but not leave you full. If, one morning, you know that you have a very busy schedule that day and won't have a chance to eat for a good five hours, you might want eggs for breakfast so that you will have the fat and protein to carry you through. If, instead, you are planning to go out to an early lunch with friends, you might want to choose something lighter in the morning, such as some fruit or cereal.

Learning to eat consciously and to treat our physical hungers with respect rather than hostility ("I wonder why I am hungry now?" rather than "I can't believe I am hungry again!") is an important part of the recovery process.

For many women who have struggled with disordered eating most of their lives, there is nothing more terrifying than the concept of eating whatever they want. They truly feel that left to their own devices, they would destroy themselves, that if they dared to trust their physical appetites, they would go spinning out of control. They need to understand that it is not their physical appetite that leads them to overeat, but the deprivation they experience in other aspects of their lives. As they learn to appease their emotional hungers with something other than food and to eat only when physically hungry, their appetites will no longer seem so dangerous.

One of the first dilemmas a woman learning to eat in accordance with her physical appetite encounters is "What do I do if I am eating something that tastes absolutely delicious and I feel full before I can finish it?" In the past, she might have said, "Tomorrow is a diet day, I better eat this now," and then quickly gobble it down. As she learns to respond to physical hunger more appropriately, she may choose instead to save that delicious food for when she feels hungry again or allow herself to select it the next time she is hungry. Eventually, she may surprise herself by eating only half a candy bar and saving the rest for later, or by having two Oreo cookies rather than the whole bag. Food then becomes just food and not something forbidden, sinful, or rewarding.

Once we are able to stop seeing food as our enemy, we find we can use it to learn more about our emotional state. We begin to see that our favorite binge foods speak to us and for us. When we learn to listen carefully and decipher what our food choices have to say, the information can be quite revealing. Certain qualities in foods can be associated with certain feelings or with the suppression of certain feelings. For example, women who crave warm foods such as soups and stews are often longing for emotional warmth in their lives. Those who crave sweets may either be missing sweetness in their lives or be trying to make themselves "sweeter." A craving for spicy foods may indicate a need for intellectual or emotional stimulation, a desire to spice up one's life. Crunchy, salty foods are often associated with frustration or the need to express anger. For many women, chocolate carries images of love or forbidden sexuality.

Playing with the symbolic meaning of food can help reveal troubling feelings that for one reason or another have been kept out of our awareness. If a woman finds herself craving a particular food and determines that she is not physically hungry, she can be certain that it is her heart basket that needs to be filled. Knowing that this food is holding an emotional charge for her, she may ask herself, "What is the feeling I don't want to feel? What might be bothering me? What feels out of balance in my life?" If this line of inner searching leads nowhere, she can then turn to the food she craves to give her some clues.

Instead of forbidding herself from eating the food or wolfing it down to quickly dispel her guilty feelings, she needs to eat it very slowly, deliberately, and consciously, asking herself with each bite, "What is it about this food that I like so much? What are the qualities I find so attractive? What is it about the taste, the texture, that is so appealing to me? What memories does it evoke?" An example of this inner dialogue might go something like this:

Q: "What is it about chocolate chip ice cream that I like so much?"

A: "I like it because it is smooth, sweet, and creamy."

Q: "Is my life feeling too rough right now, not sweet enough? Am I trying to smooth things out, make myself sweeter?"

A: "Well, I'm having a rough time in my marriage and I wish my husband were not so angry. I keep thinking that if I were sweeter, then maybe he wouldn't get angry so often."

Q: "What else is it about chocolate chip ice cream that I like?"

A: "Well, I really like the crunch of the chocolate chips in contrast to the smooth, creamy ice cream."

Q: "Am I trying to reconcile my anger toward my husband with my desire to be sweet?"

A: "I guess I don't really feel comfortable expressing my anger because he thinks I'm too bitchy."

Appreciating the way foods act as metaphors for our deepest longings and concerns can move a woman far along the path of recovery. As she pays attention to her cravings and the images they evoke, she can bring unconscious feelings and desires into the open. She can gain a better understanding of what the real issues are that she struggles with, an understanding she might not have obtained if she had continued to deny herself those foods.

By distinguishing her physical hunger from symbolic hunger, she is no longer tricked into thinking it is food she wants rather than the fulfillment of her heart's desire. She sees the illusion for what it is.

18

The Journal

Recording the Truth

*This old Korean folktale is about a woman whose husband had
returned from the war. He had been gone a long time and she was so
happy that he had returned alive and well. But he wasn't the same as
she had remembered him. He no longer laughed freely and was often
sullen and withdrawn. At times he would refuse to eat or would fly
into terrible rages that frightened her. It seemed that there was
nothing she could do to get him to laugh and love life the way he
used to.*

    *In desperation, the woman sought help from an old healer who
lived on the outskirts of her village. The healer assured the woman that
she could provide her with a potion that would restore her husband's
good humor and vitality, but the woman would have to obtain the
essential ingredient: a whisker from a living tiger. The woman was
overwhelmed by the impossibility of such a task, but the healer insisted
that without this ingredient, the potion would be worthless.*

    *The woman returned home and thought long and hard about
this task. She remembered hearing about a tiger's cave high up on the
mountain nearest her village. One night, while her husband was
sleeping, she climbed the mountain, and sure enough, as she had been*

told, there was the tiger's cave. She returned home before daylight with a plan in mind.

The next night, she climbed the mountain again, this time with a bowl of rice and a piece of meat, which she placed as near to the entrance to the cave as she dared to go. Hiding behind a bush, she watched as the tiger came out of the cave, sniffed cautiously at the bowl, and proceeded to eat. The following night she returned with another bowl of rice and meat and stood far away in the distance and watched as the tiger ate the entire contents of the bowl.

Night after night she returned with a bowl of rice and meat, each time moving closer and closer to where she placed the bowl and speaking to the tiger in a gentle, encouraging tone until one night she was close enough to the tiger that she could actually touch it. At that moment she swiftly pulled out a pair of scissors from her pocket and snipped off one of the tiger's whiskers, and with the whisker clutched tightly in her fist, she ran as fast as her legs could carry her down the mountain to the hut at the edge of the village where the healer lived. Panting, nearly out of breath, holding the whisker in her fist triumphantly in the air, she gasped, "I have it! I have the tiger's whisker. Now you can make the potion that will make my husband lively and loving again."

The healer took the whisker, inspected it for a moment, and then promptly threw it into the fire where it crackled, sizzled, and then was no more. "What have you done?" cried the woman. "Don't you know what I have been through to get that whisker?" The woman began to sob as she recounted how she had searched for the tiger's den, climbed the mountain night after night, brought food for the tiger, inched her way closer and closer to the tiger each night as he ate, spoke gentle, coaxing words even though her legs trembled with fear until she was finally able to get close enough to snip off the coveted whisker. "And now," she concluded, "it is all for nothing."

The healer looked at the woman and smiled gently. "It is not for nothing. You have done well. Remember what steps you took to tame the tiger and gain his trust. Now do the same with your husband."

For many women, a life free from obsessions with food, fat, and dieting can sometimes seem as rare and unobtainable as a tiger's whisker. Even if they knew where to find a living tiger, the thought of actually plucking one of its whiskers is nearly impossible for them to imagine. Even though they can fantasize about how life would be without their obsessions, actually living such a life seems unfathomable. Not believing they are capable of having the freedom to eat what they want without getting fat, they settle for potions that are really worthless—diets, pills, and exercise routines that bring weight loss but not freedom from the obsessions that haunt them.

The essential ingredient for true freedom is consciousness, an acute awareness, moment to moment, of who we really are and what we truly desire. It is not enough to know, in general, how we feel about our lives, our relationships, or our careers. We must be aware of our feelings and desires as they arise. And we must be willing to do what it takes to honor and acknowledge them in that moment. Journal keeping is one of the best techniques I have found for developing and maintaining this consciousness. It is a way of following and tracking our innermost thoughts and feelings while they are still being formulated, before they are ready to be shared with the world. It provides a haven from the judgments and reactions from others when we are feeling unsure of ourselves. And it can illuminate quite clearly the relationship between our thoughts and feelings and our eating behavior.

A journal that reveals the threads that connect our eating behaviors to what is going on in our lives and in our thoughts and feelings can help dispel the myth that we binge "for no particular reason," that some mysterious force comes from out of the blue and urges us to eat. When we can find those places where we have linked binge eating with frustration or ice cream with loneliness, we can find the hidden reasons for our disordered eating and can discover the areas in our lives that need to be brought into balance, that are lacking in nourishment.

The journal I recommend should contain the following information:

1. The date
2. The time you ate or drank anything
3. What you ate
4. What you were doing just before you ate
5. What you were thinking just before you ate
6. What you were feeling just before you ate
7. If you were physically hungry
8. And if you purged or got rid of the food in some way

It is important to make entries as soon as possible after eating because if too much time has passed, it can be difficult to remember not only what you had eaten but also what you had been thinking and feeling prior to eating. For this reason, many women find it helpful to use a small notebook they can carry with them.

This journal does not have to be elaborate, but it does need to be as consistent as possible. Like the woman in the story who discovered that by being consistent and persistent she could get closer to the tiger, a woman wanting freedom from food obsessions must be consistent and persistent in her attempts to draw out the real issues behind her disordered eating.

It is not unusual for a woman to discover upon starting her journal keeping that she has been harboring many negative self-judgments about her eating behavior. She may say to herself, "Oh, I can't believe I ate so much! What a pig! How disgusting!" Often the guilt and shame she feels regarding her eating behavior can interfere with her ability to be thorough or consistent with her journal entries. If so, she may find it helpful to approach this task with the attitude of a detective, a journalist, or a scientist and recognize that at this point in time, she is simply gathering data, she is collecting information to be deciphered at a later date. Even if she is binge eating every day, it's okay. Writing about these binge episodes will provide her with a multitude of clues that can help her solve the mystery of her disordered eating.

Because journal keeping is an attempt to bring the unconscious into consciousness, resistance to keeping a journal can be fierce. We tend to keep certain behavior patterns out of our awareness if they are frightening, painful, or confusing to look at. Resistance is not "bad" and we are not "lazy" or "stubborn" for not writing in our journals. When we encounter our own resistances we stumble across yet another opportunity to discover what underlies our disordered eating. But rather than scolding or berating ourselves, we need to ask with curiosity, not judgment. "I wonder why I don't want to write down what I'm eating and feeling?" "What could be getting in the way of my paying attention to what I'm doing with food?" "Are there certain feelings I'm trying not to feel?" "What am I most afraid of?" Like the woman in the story, we must speak in gentle, encouraging tones to calm our fears as we get closer and closer to our truth. And then we must sit still and listen. If we ask these questions with a gentle curiosity, the wise woman within us will reply.

Many women discover that they have a hard time getting in touch with how they are feeling. They notice their journal entries are primarily about food. If they are persistent, however, in writing down *something* to acknowledge their emotional state, such as "I'm not sure what I feel" or simply "Feeling confused," they will eventually develop greater awareness of their feelings. The more they ask themselves, "How am I feeling?," the easier it will be for them to identify their feelings with clarity and precision. As the woman in the story discovered, it was only by climbing the mountain over and over that she could achieve her goal. It is only by asking over and over "What was I feeling just before I ate?" that this level of awareness can be achieved.

After several weeks of keeping a journal, patterns will emerge. To find those patterns, look to see if there are specific times of the day when you restrict your eating. Are there times you are more likely to binge? Do you go for long periods of time without eating and then find yourself overeating? Notice if there are activities or feelings that trigger your desire to eat when you are not hungry, or situations when you don't allow yourself to eat even though you are hungry.

One woman may discover, for example, that she frequently overeats at 4:00 P.M. With close observation, she realizes that this is the time she comes home to an empty house. Not wanting to feel her loneliness, she heads straight for the refrigerator, without even questioning whether or not she is hungry. Another woman may notice that it is on those days when she is most busy and rushed that her evening meal proceeds into a binge as she turns to food to calm herself down. Some women recognize that fatigue leads to nonstop nibbling as they try to refuel, while for others connections between binge-purge episodes and fights with boyfriends or parents become obvious. Most women discover how often they eat for emotional reasons: because they are lonely, angry, bored, or nervous.

Many women develop a much better understanding of their metabolism as they review their journal entries. One woman may discover that if she goes longer than four hours without eating, she overeats. Another may realize that if she tries to eliminate carbohydrates from her diet, she sets herself up for a "carbohydrate binge" later on. Yet another woman may discover that she needs six small meals instead of three square meals a day.

Your journal keeping will help you to develop the very skills and attributes you need to overcome what may seem to be an insurmountable problem. Just as the woman in the story had to learn how to be unwavering in her commitment to healing her husband, to trust in her ability to find the tiger, to combine courage with gentle and patient encouragement so she could coax the tiger closer and get what she needed, a woman who is dedicated to healing her eating disorder must remain committed even when she is overwhelmed, persistent in her search for hidden feelings, patient with her own resistance as she gets closer to her truth, and gentle with herself as she coaxes out even the most terrifying emotions. The process of keeping a journal wherein you persistently stalk your thoughts and feelings without judgment day in and day out is what it takes to get the special ingredient, the whisker, the inner truth that can provide the healing you desperately want.

While the discovery of the specific relationships between feelings and eating patterns may ultimately provide an elixir for your disordered eating, the process of finding that special ingredient and of learning how to communicate with yourself, to pay attention to what you think and how you feel, to examine your eating behavior with curiosity instead of hostility, and to look to your body for guidance, is one that needs to be honored. Because, as the wise old healer from the story knew, it is being patient and persistent in observing yourself that you will gain trust and confidence in your inner wisdom that will serve you the rest of your life, long after you have solved your problem with disordered eating.

19

Recovery

Out of the Labyrinth

Recovery from disordered eating is about accepting the wholeness of your being. It is about accepting all of who you are, all of your emotions, thoughts, and desires, even those you may not like or those that bring discomfort. It involves recognizing that certain attributes you have viewed as liabilities are actually assets, realizing that your sensitive nature is a part of your beauty, and understanding that your uniqueness does not have to lead to isolation, rejection, and loneliness.

The Hans Christian Andersen fairy tale of The Ugly Duckling speaks to this experience:

It was summertime and a time of great beauty in the country. The sun shone warmly on an old country house, surrounded by deep canals where great burdock leaves grew so tall that children could not be seen standing upright in them. It was here in this place as wild and lonely as the thickest part of the woods that a mother duck had chosen to make her nest. She had sat on her eggs for so long that the pleasure she had felt at first was now almost gone.

At last the eggs began to crack and, one by one, the little ducklings got their first peeks at the world. Mother Duck was proud

*of her little ducklings and boasted to all the other ducks passing by
about how pretty they were.*

*Just when the mother duck thought that all of her ducklings
had hatched, she noticed that the largest egg remained in her nest.
With a weary sigh, she sat back down and waited. In time, an old
duck waddled by, inspected the egg, and announced that it was a
turkey's egg. She suggested the mother duck abandon it and busy
herself teaching her ducklings to swim.*

*Mother Duck persisted, however, and at long last the great egg
began to crack and a new life tumbled out into the world. "Oh,"
thought the mother duck, "how large and ugly this one is. This is a
great, strong creature. None of the others are at all like it. I wonder
what it is?"*

*The next day Mother Duck took her new family for a swim. All
the ducklings jumped into the water and swam quite easily, even the
large and ugly one. "Well, it must not be a turkey," Mother Duck
thought. "Although it is not as beautiful as my others, it is rather
attractive in its own way. I will accept it as my own and teach it the
ways of the world."*

*But the other ducks were not as tolerant or accepting as the
mother duck. They bit, kicked, pecked at, and teased the poor creature
mercilessly. Even the ugly duckling's brothers and sisters behaved
unkindly, constantly saying, "May the cat eat you, you ugly thing."
And eventually, the mother duck, distressed by all the problems caused
from having such an ugly one, found herself wishing to be rid of the
duckling.*

*The poor duckling, overwhelmed with feelings of rejection, ran
away, not knowing where to go but desperately wanting some reprieve
from the mistreatment. Feeling very tired and sorrowful, the duckling
reached a wide moor where some wild ducks lived. "You are so ugly,"
they said, "but you are welcome to stay here as long as you do not*

plan to marry into our family." The poor duckling had never even thought of marriage!

Shortly thereafter, a couple of wild geese came to the moor. They took one look at the strange new duckling and with a sarcastic tone said, "You are so ugly that we like you. Why don't you come with us to the next moor where you may be lucky enough to find someone to marry you." While the duckling was considering this proposition, the air was suddenly filled with gunshots and geese lay dead on the ground. A whole flock of geese flew up from the rushes and hunters with dogs splashed through the mud.

The panicked duckling came face to face with a growling, ferocious dog who stared and then splashed away without attacking. "I guess I should be thankful," the duckling sighed in relief. "I am so ugly, not even a dog will bite me."

And so the duckling ran on and on, through fierce winds brought on by a storm that was brewing, over fields and meadows, arriving by nightfall at a wretched hut that was barely standing. Desperate to escape from the storm that was growing worse and worse, the exhausted duckling crept into the hut.

In this room lived an old woman with her tomcat and her hen who she loved as her own children. The next morning the cat began to meow and the hen began to cackle when they saw their new guest. The old woman, whose vision was failing, thought the large duckling was a fat duck who had lost its way. "Oh, this is good," she said. "If this is not a drake, I shall now have duck's eggs. We must wait and see."

Now, the cat envisioned himself to be the master of the house and the hen saw herself as the mistress. Together they imagined themselves to be the keepers of the truth. When the duckling suggested a different way of viewing things, the hen became hostile.

"Can you lay eggs?" she asked.

"No," replied the duckling.

"Then you should hold your tongue," she said with contempt.

"Can you purr?" asked the cat.

"No."

"Well, then your opinion is worthless," the cat said smugly.

"But I love to swim," said the duckling. "It is so wonderful when the cool waters close over your head and you plunge to the bottom."

"That is a weird sort of pleasure," responded the hen. "You must be crazy."

"I think you do not understand me," said the duckling.

"What? You think yourself wiser than us? You should be thankful for all the kindness we have shown you and be appreciative that you have friends such as us who will tell you the truth, however unpleasant it may be for you."

The duckling, realizing that this, too, was not a welcoming place to stay, went away. Autumn came and the leaves turned gold and brown. The wind swirled them around, and the air grew cold. One evening as the duckling shivered on a pond, feeling cold and lonely, a large flock of birds rose from the brush. What magnificent birds they were! Their plumage was a dazzling white and they had long, slender necks. They were swans. They uttered a loud cry as they spread out their splendid wings and flew away. Upon seeing and hearing them, the duckling felt a strange sensation and, although they were gone in an instant, the memory of those noble birds remained.

When winter came it was bitterly cold, so cold that the poor duckling had to swim round and round just to keep from freezing. Every night the opening in the frozen pond became smaller and smaller and the duckling eventually collapsed from exhaustion.

The next morning a peasant happened to pass by and see the half-dead duckling. He broke the ice and carried the duckling home to his wife. When the duckling's health was restored, the children *wanted to play, but the duckling ran from them in fear, expecting more harassment. Flying first into the milk pail, then into the butter tub and flour barrel with the peasant's wife screaming hysterically, the duckling panicked and fled into the moor.*

There, the sun was shining, birds were singing, and apple trees were in blossom. Spring had returned. Everything was lovely, fresh, and full of promise.

Out of the thicket came three beautiful swans. They displayed their feathers proudly and swam ever so lightly on the water. The duckling felt that same sensation, first experienced the autumn before and decided, "I must swim out to those glorious creatures. Even though they are sure to attack me for my ugliness."

The swans saw the ugly duckling swimming toward them and turned to greet the sad, frightened creature. The duckling bowed low and was startled to see a reflection of another swan in the water—not a plump, ugly, gray bird but a beautiful swan!

The swans swam near and stroked their new friend with their beaks, and the duckling, I mean swan, felt joy that knew no bounds. Children came down to the lake, threw bits of bread to the swans, and said, "Look, there is a new one, so young and so beautiful."

The young swan's heart glowed as she thought, "I never imagined such happiness when I was the ugly, despised duckling."

Like the ugly duckling, women who struggle with disordered eating know all to well the experience of the outcast. As children, they often had feelings of not quite belonging, of being different from others, and of being excluded because of that differentness. Because expression of their strong intuitive, instinctual nature was often at odds with the values of our culture, their families didn't quite know what to do with such precocious, curious children who threatened to "rock the boat." Desperately wanting a sense of belonging, many of these children tried to cope by being the best "duck" they could be and by denying or hiding their differentness. Others outwardly rebelled and tried to get away from a family that didn't seem to understand them. Either way, a steep price was paid. Those who denied their inner nature became addicted to stuffing down their true feelings with food or gravitated to restrictive diets that could distract them from their intuition. Those who rebelled covertly, expressing their anger through the rejection of food, often placed their very lives in danger. Those who rebelled overtly found that the sting of rejection and the ache of loneliness could be soothed symbolically by compulsive eating or by food obsessions that eventually entrapped them.

Recovery from disordered eating requires that a woman come to terms with the uniqueness of her being. Like the ugly duckling, she must embark on a journey to find herself, to find her place in this world. Although there is nothing wrong with being a duck, trying to act like a duck when you are really a swan can be frustrating and painful because no matter what you do, it will never be just right and you will be left with feelings of failure or of not being good enough.

A woman on this journey must persist, like the duckling, even in the face of great difficulty. She must leave situations that are abusive, and not stay where she is subject to shame or ridicule. Just as the duckling felt compelled to leave when the cat and the hen insisted that their worldview was the only correct one, a woman in search of herself must also not associate with those who demand conformity. She must not sell out by settling for security in exchange for acceptance. She must press on until she finds those who recognize and accept who she really is, those who can share her delight in diving deep into the waters of her emotions. She must persevere until she can see the beauty of her own reflection.

When a woman who travels the labyrinth of recovery comes to the center of her being, she discovers who she is and lets go of who she or others think she *should* be. She retrieves all those parts of herself that had been lost or discarded and finds wholeness. Her task then is to wind her way back out and weave this new sense of herself into a new way of being in the world. As she begins this leg of the journey, renewed yet inexperienced, she may find the winding path out as arduous as the one she came in on. With its many twists, curves, and hairpin turns, it may sometimes appear to her as though she is backsliding, that things are getting worse rather than better. She may feel frustrated over not making her way as easily or as smoothly as she thinks she should, and become impatient with herself for not getting "better" as quickly as she had expected.

When a woman becomes more and more aware of feelings she has blocked, when she allows herself to feel the full force of her anger, sadness, or loneliness, it may seem to her as though she is getting worse because she is *feeling* worse. She may not realize that she is simply feeling *more*. The emotions that surface first are usually the ones with which we are most uncomfortable, and often the ones that are most in need of awareness and expression. When they begin to emerge, it is important that we not evaluate them harshly or subject them to judgment from others. They need to be felt, accepted, and expressed so they can pass and not get in the way.

A woman who has developed a long term habit of blocking her feelings with compulsive eating or food obsessions may find herself wanting to binge more or starve more than ever as her long-buried feelings begin to surface. If this happens, it can be very frightening and she may be tempted to abandon her recovery process. For this reason, it might be a good idea to seek guidance from a therapist or support group, a safe place where her feelings can be expressed and honored.

If a woman can find the support she needs in order to experience, accept, and express her feelings, she need not worry that her obsessions with food and eating will worsen. She will recognize that sometimes there is "lag time" between the emergence of her feelings and the development of new skills for coping with them, but as she learns to respond to her feelings in new ways, her urge to binge, starve, diet, or exercise compulsively will begin to subside.

As part of this process, a woman must learn that there are real differences between thinking and behavior and that both must be honored and given time to change. She may, for example, find herself able to understand rather quickly what she is doing with food but still unable to respond any differently to the emotional issues that arise. Learning to respond differently to feelings takes time and practice and every woman needs to be aware of this. Harsh self-judgments like "I should know better," and "What's wrong with me?" will not help at all. They'll only get in the way. More than ever, this needs to be a time for kindness and compassion toward herself as she stumbles along, trying to find her way.

Before a woman can complete the process of recovery, she must pass through stages of self-awareness and learn new skills, just as the duckling had to go through all the seasons to develop the strength and maturity she needed to find her place in the world.

As a woman journeys out of the labyrinth toward recovery from disordered eating, she may find herself walking a path that resembles a backward spiral. She can expect to keep retracing her steps over and over until she finds those moments when she is responding to her thoughts and feelings by eating (or not eating). She must work toward bringing her general understanding of the connection between food and feelings closer and closer to those specific incidents that trigger her disordered eating. Each time she retraces her steps she goes to a different level of awareness.

She begins with being able to see patterns. After having kept a journal for a few weeks, she may notice that her telephone conversations with her mother are usually followed by binges. This pattern had not been obvious until she had observed and recorded her behavior for some time. While she may now be able to see what is triggering her binges, she can only do so after some time has already passed.

As she continues on, her self-awareness becomes more immediate. She realizes, as she is writing in her journal, "I know why I just binged. I was upset with my mom."

Eventually she finds herself aware of the feeling she is trying to stuff down at the very moment she is doing so: she had a conversation with her mother, became upset over something that her mother said, hung up the phone, and proceeded to binge. While in the middle of bingeing, she realizes, "I know I'm doing this because I'm mad at my mother." But she is unable to stop the binge process because the wheels have already been set in motion and there is just too much momentum. Rather than judging herself for not being able to stop bingeing, she needs at this point to appreciate the new awareness that she's achieved.

As she persists on her way toward greater self-awareness, she finds herself becoming aware of her feelings *just before* she starts to binge: she talks to her mother on the phone, hangs up feeling angry and frustrated, and reaches for something to eat. She is aware in that moment that the reason she wants to eat is that she is angry at her mother, not because she is physically hungry. She may decide to binge anyway, but now she knows full well that it's not physical nourishment she is craving.

Once again, this is not a place for self-recrimination. This is not a time to say to herself, "What's wrong with me? I *knew* I wasn't hungry!" Instead she needs to recognize that she is now at the stage of understanding what it is she is feeling just before the binge begins. Rather than berate herself, she ought to acknowledge how far she has come. She has finally arrived at the crossroads, a place where she has a *choice*. That she may choose to eat instead of expressing her anger toward her mother is fine. Her skills for dealing with her anger any other way might not be fully developed.

At least she is at a point where she can choose consciously how she wants to respond to her feelings.

It may take some time for her to move out of this stage. There may be many moments when, fully aware that she is about to eat for emotional reasons, she says to herself, "I don't care. I'm going to eat anyway." As she begins to be more accepting of her feelings and learns more direct ways of expressing them, she will begin to discover that she has many more choices than she ever used to have.

As time goes on, she may explore different ways of expressing her feelings. She might call a friend to talk about how she feels, or she might let her feelings spew out in a nasty letter to her mother that she doesn't intend to send. She might go in the shower and yell obscenities. She might call her mother back and, using the assertiveness formula (see chapter 16), let her mother know how her comments affected her.

At last, she arrives at the place where she becomes aware of her angry feelings *while* she is still talking to her mother, and a little voice inside of her says, "If I don't say something now, as soon as I hang up I'm going to want to binge." If by this time she has had enough experience expressing her feelings assertively, she has an idea of how to respond to them *in the moment.* And so she might say, "You know, when you say blah, blah, blah, I get upset because I get the impression that you're talking down to me."

She is now able to head the binge behavior off at the pass. Since she is experiencing her feelings the moment they arise and expressing them directly, they can pass. She no longer needs to binge in an attempt to block them out of her awareness.

So this is what a woman can expect as she spirals backward, around and around, on her way out of the labyrinth toward freedom from food obsessions. She discovers it's not enough to know that holding back feelings can lead to compulsive eating. She must also learn to be aware of what those feelings are in the very moment she is reaching for the chocolate chip cookies or that extra slice of pizza. It's not enough to be able to name the conflicts that lie at the root of her excessive dieting. She must do what it takes to resolve them. It's not enough to identify the feelings that trigger bingeing and purging. She must respond to those emotions in a way that brings the nourishment or relief she craves.

When a woman continues along the path of recovery she might become discouraged at the pace she must travel. As she looks for physical evidence of her progress and fails to see immediate changes in her appearance or in her eating, it may seem as though she is getting nowhere. She needs to remember that much of what she has accomplished has been in the emotional and mental realms and has not yet manifested in the physical world. In time, it will.

Imagine walking frequently down a street where a building is being constructed. Day after day, for many months, you pass by what seems to be an empty lot. And then one day, rather suddenly, up goes some scaffolding and before you know it, a huge building appears. It seems as though it went up overnight.

This is not unlike the recovery process from disordered eating. For a long time it may seem as though nothing is happening, that no progress is being made. But in actuality, much is happening. It is just that it's been taking place in the realm of the invisible. As with the building, much time needs to go into preparation, into planning and laying a foundation that can fully support a new structure, a structure that can last over time. Once you have laid the foundation by understanding the causes of your disordered eating and have developed the skills you need to face the stresses that life can bring, a new way of relating to food will surely follow.

A woman cannot be rushed. When she is able to grow slowly into herself, her body has the time to adjust. As she learns to recognize, accept, and express her feelings and allows her body to tell her when and what to eat, when to exercise and when to rest, her body will slowly, but steadily, find the weight that is right for her and that most fully expresses her natural, feminine beauty.

20

Storytime

The Tales of Three Women

Storytellers speak in the language of myth and metaphor. They tell us a truth that is not literal but symbolic. If we hear the stories with only our outer ear, they can seem absurd and untrue, but when listened to with our inner ear, they convey an inner truth that can be understood on a very personal level and absorbed. In this way, they help us connect with our inner world, our own mythic reality.

When we hear the wisdom in stories, we are listening to a language of symbols that speaks to inner truths. This language of symbol and metaphor helps us recognize the existence of deeper meanings and truths. We can begin to see that our own inner truth is often obfuscated by our surface realities and that our deeper longings are often tucked behind our more visible compulsions. We can see how food is a metaphor for emotional and spiritual nourishment, how eating is an attempt to respond to inner hungers for attention, acknowledgment, affection, or appreciation.

Because the story of our life becomes our life, it is important for a woman recovering from disordered eating to review her life's story and to reframe it with a new understanding of her self and her behavior. In the telling of her story, she can begin to hear her inner truths as they emerge from behind the surface details. She can glimpse the symbolism of her obsession with thinness, her hunger for chocolate, her need to stuff herself. She can speak of struggles with conflict, identity, and desire, not in the hard light of reason, but in the light of the moon, which can softly and gently illuminate her truth.

Here are three tales told by women whose disordered eating behavior is now behind them. They are tales of damaged families and caring families, tales of great misfortune and wondrous gifts. Listen with your inner ear for the truth as it resonates with your own story.

A woman, now a therapist in her early thirties, tells a story about her long struggle for approval and acceptance. Unlike the ugly duckling, the "differentness" she felt as a child was no great mystery. No secret had been made of the fact that she had been adopted. Although she was told how "special" she was to have been "chosen" to be a member of her family, she learned at a young age that this coveted specialness could be maintained in her mother's eyes only through great achievement. By doing, not by being.

She became a competitive swimmer. State champion, no less. At the pool, she learned to throw up to remove butterflies from her stomach, to eliminate any feelings that might interfere with winning and to distract herself from feelings about her mother's recently diagnosed breast cancer, from feelings of never being good enough, special enough to please her.

"Ever since I was fourteen, my mother was supposed to die, which got in the way of my expressing any anger toward her. I couldn't! It was always, 'your poor, sick mother. You can't tell her the truth about how you're really thinking and feeling because she could be dead tomorrow.' I had to live with that all my life."

When she left for college on a swimming scholarship, her occasional binge-purge episodes developed into a full-scale eating disorder. *"At first I felt so free, like now I can be whoever I want, but I didn't know how. I didn't know how to be me."*

Not knowing where to look in her search for her true self, she focused on her outer appearance and obsessed about her weight. *"Although I weighed only a hunded and fifteen pounds I felt like I had to work frenetically, at a feverish pitch, to keep the weight off. It felt like there was something I had to keep at bay. If I just let things be, something bad was going to overtake me."*

In her reflections, she recognized that the vague "something" she didn't understand at the time was the emergence of her female sexuality. Food deprivation was the only way she knew to control the strong instincts that threatened to overwhelm her.

"I had such strong urges. I wanted to have sex with just about every good-looking man I saw. But I was more interested in the feeling of power than anything else. I think things got distorted somehow, like I had this image that I could 'get' someone with my sexuality. I tried to be like a guy—to use my sexuality to get power, to win someone over. I really went for the shock value, flirting and talking about sex, like this is no 'biggie' to me. It was a way to try to disarm guys and also feel like I was bonding with them, like I was 'just one of the guys.' And the eating disorder became even more crazy as I started acting out sexually.

"I became the first woman to rush a fraternity instead of a sorority. I rejected my feminine nature because I saw that the power was with the masculine, and I wanted to go where the power was. And I hurt myself terribly because I rejected myself."

She plunged into the darkness of depression. She had ventured out in search of her individual self and had lost her way. Without the light of the moon to guide her, without a way of honoring her feminine nature, it had become buried beneath an emphasis on masculine qualities of doing, accomplishing, competing, succeeding. "Power over others" was the only power she could recognize.

In desperation, she sought help from a therapist and began her journey into the labyrinth. She started to see that her struggle with food was related to *"my enmeshed relationship with my mother and that my acting out was an attempt to separate from the feminine that I hated. I had so much rage toward my mom at that time that I saw her as someone I never wanted to be. She was so controlling and mean to me, and it was so awful having a relationship with her at that time. She would put out love, and as soon as I would respond, she would take it away, so I always felt like if I attempted to get close to her, I would get my ass kicked. So I worked really hard to figure out how to be good enough to please her, but it was never enough. Never, never, never. I never felt she had any confidence in me. Never felt she respected me. I think that is why I acted out so strongly against the feminine."*

As she continued on her path toward recovery, retrieving lost and disowned parts of herself along the way, she eventually came to a place where she needed to descend deep into the darkest part of her being.

"I began working on my incest. When I was nine, ten, eleven, my brother was in high school. He was going into puberty at that age and he had no friends, so he acted out on me sexually. I had a lot of rage at my brother all those years and he finally stopped just as I was turning twelve, when I burst out with my rage. It's interesting that a year later my eating disorder started. I'd always known about the incest with my brother. It was something in the back of my mind that had never gone away. But I didn't tell my folks until I got into therapy and my brother admitted everything and helped pay for my therapy."

As she proceeded to weave her way in and out of the labyrinth, she learned the language of metaphor.

"I began to see that my eating disorder was there to tell me something, that every time I puked there was something that needed to be said, but I wasn't able to find the words. That was so valuable for me. I remember standing there, pacing around my house going, 'Okay,

what is it?!' I would have to talk out loud and pace the house and I would pace and pace and pace and pace.

"I noticed that what I binged on was always sweet always ice cream, cake, cookies—sweet, creamy things—a symbol for the sweet, nurturing mother that I wanted but didn't feel like I could really have."

She began to listen to her body and quiet her mind.

"I learned how to be conscious when I eat, to just ask my body what's going on. How to slow down and be aware. I used to rush around all the time. I started doing meditation. I could not believe what it was like to have a quiet mind! Because my mind had never been quiet. I was always berating myself, 'I can't believe you just went to the store and bought ice cream. I thought you said you weren't going to do that!' When I started learning to meditate it was like a little slice of heaven. And that slice of heaven was so much more fulfilling than a slice of pie or cake.

"I got turned on to the idea of the Goddess, that there is strength in the feminine, in the quiet stillness of just being and feeling. Before, I always had to be doing. I had to race. I had to be competitive."

As she gained greater acceptance of her intuitive and emotionally sensitive nature, she was able to address the conflicts with her mother who was much more emotionally reserved and approached life in a more practical, methodical, linear manner.

"Of course, resolving my relationship with my mother was hard work. I had to be assertive and to continually confront her when I felt her rejecting me or trying to control me. I had to do the 'broken record' over and over. Three months before she died, after struggling with cancer for seventeen years, she said finally, 'I don't worry about you anymore.' That was the greatest gift she could have given me. I realized that that's where all her anger was coming from. She didn't have any confidence in me because I approached things so differently from her. She felt like she had to protect me and would get so angry when I would do things my way."

On her journey toward recovery from disordered eating, this woman learned to honor and embrace her feminine nature, accept her sexuality, listen to her body, resolve her issues with her brother and mother, and find her true self.

"And I did it! When I resolved those issues seven years ago, I was pretty much finished. I never went back.

"I know my recovery is complete because when my mom died recently, I didn't go back to using food to cope with or block my feelings. I used food consciously. I ate chocolate chip cookies because they reminded me of her, baking cookies and stuff, but I didn't go to that place of being desperate or crazy with my relationship with food. I felt overwhelmed and out of control with the loss of my mom, but that was where I was supposed to be. Before, when really stressful things had happened, I would find myself in that unconscious place with food instead of dealing with what I was supposed to be dealing with. For me it was very triumphant to work with my feelings directly and not use food as a vehicle to try to deny them."

Another woman, a young mother, shares her story of a hunger she did not know the name of, of a longing for attention, acknowledgment, and appreciation so great it nearly killed her.

"In my family, we all had our own separate lives. When I was at home, I was by myself. I was in my room or watching TV. I can't really remember much interaction with my parents. I can't picture them with me at home, asking me questions or anything. I felt really lonely I guess. But I was used to it. The only one I felt close to was my brother, who was a year older. We always talked about everything."

When she was still a young child, she developed a passion for music.

"I taught myself to play piano on my neighbor's piano. I played whenever I could, like when people I babysat for had a piano. Sometimes I would go down to the church at night where I would put on

headphones and listen to a song I liked, playing it over and over until I got every note perfectly.

"One day I came home from school with a flute I had been given in band class. It was an awesome flute. I remember thinking it must have cost a hundred dollars! And as I practiced in my room I got better and better and would play louder and louder, wanting someone to hear the beautiful music, until my mother yelled, 'Shut the door!' "

Like the child in the story about the emperor's new clothes, she was a very perceptive and sensitive child. But her perceptions were never acknowledged or validated. And so she thought something was wrong with her—something was wrong with the way she thought and felt.

"I always thought I was weird, like I just didn't fit in, like I was this strange person. My parents were nice people and they seemed happy. They never talked about anything being wrong, but I always had this feeling that things weren't right in my family. My father could be quiet and moody, but there's no specific thing that ever happened I can think of or point to that caused my disordered eating. My parents always said they never did anything and they're right, they didn't do anything. I think that's the point.

"Things just didn't seem right, ever. I found out a couple of years ago that my younger sister was being molested by a teenage boy back then. I don't know if my parents knew, but being so sensitive, I probably sensed something.

"At school I just felt like I was different from everybody, and everything that happened to me felt catastrophic. I was easily overwhelmed with just normal things like getting lost in the hallway on the first day of school. I had a panic attack. I just knew I wasn't normal. I was very shy and I think I had some kind of learning disorder.

"In junior high it seemed like I lived in my own private little world. I have all these memories of thinking that 'I'm just weird.' I wasn't popular because I was too shy, and I didn't put myself at risk

by hanging out with others. I was always really nice to people who were mean to me."

Without a sense of belonging, her loneliness grew. And when her body began to change into the body of a woman, she lost the only closeness she had known.

"At this time my brother and I stopped being close. I remember when we were around thirteen, Dad had to go buy him a jock strap and Mom had to get me a bra, and we would compare and check them out and laugh and giggle. We would stay up late watching videos together, talking, and eating cereal because Mom and Dad just didn't care. We could stay up as late as we wanted to.

"But then things changed. He got friends that made me feel weird. Even though we still spent time together, we didn't really talk. We would go to movies or shopping, but it wasn't the same.

"Right around there is when I started my eating disorder. Knowing me, I probably heard about it from TV. I remember watching Fame *and this girl on it had an eating disorder and she got all of this attention. I started out by just not eating all the time. I was naturally skinny already, but I wanted to be as skinny as I could be. I wanted people to know I was sick."*

Unable to get the attention she needed but didn't know how to get, she became desperate.

"I spent about two years starving myself. I didn't get any attention for it, though, until one day I walked home from school and passed out on my bed. My mom went up into my room to talk to me because that day two of my friends from school had called my mom and told her I was sick 'cause I wasn't eating. She asked me if I was okay and when I didn't answer she put her hand under my nose and saw I wasn't breathing. She panicked and called an ambulance. My heart had stopped and my dad had to give me CPR.

"I stayed in the hospital for a while and then got transferred to the psychiatric unit. My parents were there a lot and I felt really good

like 'I've got the attention now.' The staff asked a lot of questions but it really didn't do much good because I was trying to be sick, but trying not to act like I wanted to be sick. I wouldn't give them honest answers to the questions they asked me because I wanted to stay sick. I remember a couple of times my whole family came for these sessions but nothing ever came of it. That was it. They pumped me up in weight and then I was shipped out."

Then, as fate would have it, she found love.

"*I met Davis, a boy two years older than me, shortly after getting out of the hospital. In our relationship, Davis was always the boss and I just did what he wanted, but that's what I needed then. He gave me a lot of attention, all the time.*"

But rather than living happily ever after, she found herself ill-equipped to cope with the conflicts and feelings an intimate relationship can bring.

"*I gave up on being anorexic and became bulimic. I developed a habit of throwing up, that was just how I lived my life. I didn't know any other way to deal with feelings that came up. I didn't know how to eat when I was hungry or stop when I was full. With Davis, I had sex for the first time, and even though he was the only guy I wanted, I was uncomfortable about being sexual. I think my eating disorder at that time was about blocking out everything that made me uncomfortable and sex was one of those things.*"

When Davis joined the military, she dropped out of school to marry him and they moved out of their small town. It was at this time she received the news that her brother had been killed in a car accident. "*I just lost it, crying and screaming, I couldn't believe it.*" But when she went home for the funeral she acted as though she was "just fine" and didn't cry. She had learned to distrust her own sensitivity and to deny her feelings. She knew how to harden herself to her own suffering. She stopped talking about her brother and refused ever to mention his name again.

Shortly thereafter, she had a baby and plummeted down, down into a deep depression. She felt nothing but numbness. No sorrow, no anger. No joy, no pleasure, no love. Only fatigue.

"I would stay up and clean the house and wash the dishes, and vacuum and then I couldn't fall asleep. I was just wiped out. And there wasn't anyone to help me. I thought I would go berserk. I thought I would die from tiredness, and I couldn't tell my family because they wouldn't believe me—they would just think I was trying to get attention or something."

"To feel some relief, I began eating just so I could throw up, not like before when I would eat and throw up if I felt full. And Davis never knew about the bulimia. Never. Even though we had been married six years, I kept it hidden."

She remembers her first steps into recovery began with her speaking her truth, with somehow finding the words to speak the unspeakable.

"One morning, Davis and I were going to go for a walk and something took over, like it wasn't even me talking, I could hear my voice, but it didn't seem like it was me. And I just said, 'I think I need to go get some help.' And he said, 'Why?' And I said, 'Cause I'm still kinda sick.' He said, 'What do you mean?' And I said, 'With eating, I'm still sick.' He said, 'What do you do? Aren't you eating?' And I said, 'I'm eating too much and I kinda throw it up.' I couldn't believe I said it! As we walked, he asked all these questions and I told him everything, like I was on autopilot. I knew if I told him, I would have to get help."

She began her journey by redefining herself, by reviewing her life's story within the framework of a deeper understanding and acceptance of her intuitive, sensitive nature.

"I told my therapist every single reason I thought I was weird, why I thought that I couldn't be a normal person 'cause I saw things this way and I felt this way. And one by one these things were explained and I found out I wasn't weird and unacceptable. I knew I

had an eating disorder but had thought I had no reason to be this way because my family was so normal."

From this place of acceptance she began to sing her song, the sweet song of her truth.

"When I started talking to Davis, it was really helpful. He was so open and honest. When I struggled to tell him how I felt, he would just listen or ask questions until he could say, 'Oh, okay, now I understand. What can I do?' I had to learn to tell him the truth about everything that bothered me and stop trying to keep him from being hurt. I had to express my fears that my daughter was developmentally delayed because I was a neglectful mother and my anger about having to deal with more than just regular childhood issues. At times I had to stand up to him when I felt he wasn't right."

As she made her way on this path toward recovery, she sometimes felt overwhelmed by trying to find the feelings she had repressed, the issues she needed to resolve. But she persisted, putting one foot in front of the other.

"When I first started therapy, I was really scared. How was I ever going to figure out everything that was bothering me? It seemed like I had such a big load. I had all these different problems, and it was just overwhelming to sit and think. How am I supposed to know what's wrong? I have so many different things bothering me. But now it's not a burden to think about what's wrong because I've taken care of all those old feelings, and I don't have such a big pile to dig through. I don't have to worry about getting through this one thing to get to the next thing and then there'll be another thing. Now it's just taking care of business when it comes up and not procrastinating."

She began to trust her intuition and receive the pearls of wisdom her feelings brought.

"I learned to trust myself and my perceptions of other people. Now I don't doubt myself, my sensations and premonitions, or any single feeling I have. I know I can trust them because I've been right. I don't need to use food to distract myself from knowing what I know

195

or to convince myself that I'm wrong. When I go through my day, I'm not unconscious. I'm awake and I'm hearing exactly what people are saying to me. My sensitivity is a strength, and I can use it to keep me safe from people who are not caring of me.

"What I've noticed is that when people say, 'You're too sensitive,' they're annoyed because I'm so perceptive. And it doesn't matter if I'm oversensitive, because sometimes that's a good thing. I don't worry about anybody judging me for it anymore because I can respect it in myself. So it doesn't matter if somebody says, 'You're too sensitive,' because I am, and I'm proud of it because it keeps me safe and very honest.

"I learned that all of my feelings are okay because they are mine. And I can't control them. I just need to feel them and express them. I learned to accept who I am, to set boundaries, and to assert myself. It sounds so simple but it was a lot of work."

As she made her way deep into the center of her self and wound her way back out into the world, her journal was her trusty companion.

"Keeping a journal really helped make me aware of my feelings and more conscious of myself in a lot of ways. When I wrote in my journal, I really focused on what I was thinking and feeling. I realized the way I had been living was cut off from who I was. I wasn't connected to myself. I wasn't conscious. It's hard to explain, but I had been conditioned, somehow, to do and think and feel and act without listening to my inner voice, my inner knowing. It was just bypassed somehow. I was acting and eating and throwing up without being aware of who I was and what I wanted.

"While writing in my journal, I could practice paying attention and practice thinking and feeling. For instance, I would write about how when I was a kid I didn't get much love and then I would feel sad, and then I would learn that's what sad feels like. Other times I would feel stressed out and write about feeling stressed out rather than go eat cake or pizza. Pizza was a big thing for me because I learned that when I crave pizza, I need a lot of attention."

By paying attention to her physical sensations, she began to appreciate the innate wisdom of her body.

"I learned how to find my physical hunger by eating two bites and checking in with my body, waiting until my stomach told me to eat. That was a gigantic insight, that I could wait to eat until my stomach told me to! I remember the first time I felt it; it wasn't quite a growl but almost like a little sensation in my stomach. Now, it's not stressful to actually have my stomach say, 'I'm hungry.' I don't have to worry about it all the time, like 'My gosh, I'm going to have to eat pretty soon.' I can enjoy eating now. It's a normal experience.

"I still have certain times that I might not be hungry and I start thinking about food, and all I do right away is go, 'Wait a minute, my stomach's not growling, why am I thinking about food?' And it's not so complicated to realize something else is going on—I might be emotionally, not physically hungry."

With her newfound confidence in her self, her body, and her feelings, she returned to school, earned her G.E.D., and joined a women's therapy group for disordered eating. There, she confronted her fears of rejection. *"When I started group, it was very, very scary because I'm not a very social person. I wasn't used to talking to people. It took about six months to get me there. But when I started talking in group, I found out that people didn't laugh at me. They didn't think I was stupid because I talked a certain way. I had always just assumed that I don't talk right, that I go on, or that I talk about stupid things. This is what I had been telling myself every day of my life. It was just so awful. From group, I started finding out that I was pretty cool."*

As she made her way toward the gateway leading out of the labyrinth, *"I thought, 'Fine, now I'm in therapy and learning how not to use food,' but I still was throwing up once in a while. I decided, 'I've got to find some kind of motivation to stop throwing up' because I was learning other things to do in group and then sometimes going home and throwing up anyway. It was scary to let go of it because I had been doing it for so long. So I decided I was going to set a date because this is what had always worked for me when I was a teenager, except back then I used to say, 'On this date I'm going to lose this much weight.' But now, with all the new skills I had, I could use this approach for other purposes.*

"I set the date for January 1st at 12:01 A.M. I wasn't really throwing up much before this date, but I said to myself, 'I'm going to get it all over with now,' and I threw up a candy cane at 11:59 and that was it. The ball dropped.

"And then I went and sat down and wrote in my journal. I was all by myself. Nobody but me knew I was doing this. I had been living all my life for others for so long, but this belonged to me. It was like my own special ritual. I did it for myself and I didn't have to tell anyone at all."

She discovered how to see through the illusion of her food cravings and how to decode the messages they bring.

"Before I started back to school, I began to notice I was eating at times I wasn't hungry. I would be hungry for four different foods all at once and was trying to please all my cravings at the same time. I realized later that I was also in the middle of trying to figure out if I wanted to stay home and take care of my child full-time, go to college, get a job, or have another baby. Four different choices. Four different foods. My trying to decide what to eat was really my trying to decide what to do with my life. I realized then that I now have the tools to figure this out on my own!"

She exited the labyrinth and enrolled in a community college. On her journey of recovery she had found a new vision of herself, one that included respect for her innermost thoughts, feelings, and desires. And she found the attention she had been starving for her whole life.

"I live every day paying attention to who I am, learning what I like. I don't worry about what other people think. I have learned to stay focused on myself and pay attention to others at the same time.

"It's really not about food at all. I never used to give myself time to think about what I really wanted. Like before, I would think I wanted cake, but I really didn't. I wanted a hug. Now I can tell the difference."

A third woman, with a growing career in public relations and communications, tells a story that is not unlike the story of the Princess and the Goddess. She lost her mother at age twelve, not to death, however, but to alcohol.

"I basically stopped growing emotionally when my mother became an alcoholic. Up to that point, I had had a wonderfully happy childhood. I was very precocious. I was very bright and knew I was bright. I couldn't have cared less about my appearance. That was not an issue with me.

"And then when my mom started drinking, she attacked me. Because she did not know how to deal with her emotions, she took all of her rage out on me. The pattern was she would drink every night and by dinnertime she was just attacking me with her obsession of the day: I said something grammatically incorrect or I wasn't home at four o'clock. It was never about important things, it was not about the fact that I wasn't doing my homework or anything like that, but it was nitpicky stuff about something I had said or that I didn't smile and shake someone's hand properly during the day. It was some obsession that she would fixate on all night long and chase me through the house, room to room, and come in with this crazed look on her face. I was a normally a very quiet person but she would hammer at me until I just flew into a rage, a screaming rage in her face every night."

The fairy tale had ended. Her mother was no longer the kind, loving queen and she was no longer a princess.

"Everything about me for her was wrong. She definitely had in mind the daughter she wanted and I didn't fit that bill at all. If I tried really hard I could, but just being who I was wasn't acceptable to her."

To soothe the grief she felt over the loss of the nurturing mother she once knew, she turned to food.

"I remember going down into the kitchen and making really odd concoctions of sugar and lemon juice and whipped cream and sneaking a lot of food up to my bedroom."

She felt isolated and alone within her own family and was blamed and shamed for feeling and expressing her anger over the situation.

"She never did this with my brothers. She occasionally did it with my dad, but with him she would be all moody and passive-aggressive. With me, it was very overt. Everybody would see this, that she was on me, riding me, but nobody would say, 'Mom, cut it out' or 'Mary, cut it out' and then suddenly I would explode and they would say, 'Oh, there you go again. You're out of control.'

"And I became very fearful of my anger because I never learned how to express it properly. People always told me how sweet I was and how quiet I was, and I would think, 'You've never seen me. I am capable of hari-kari.'"

Unlike the child in the story of the Emperor's New Clothes, her attempts to speak the truth were not appreciated by her father or brothers.

"I kept saying, 'This is crazy! Mom's drunk. She's out of control,' and they said, 'This is the way it is, let's just live with it.' Having a very sensitive nature, I could pick up that things weren't right and my family was so messed up and so hurting. But when I tried to voice that, everybody kept blaming me for being the one who stirred everything up, and to this day I know they look at me as though I'm not quite right.

"So I used food to tune out. Food and television were my drugs. My pattern was, I would sit down with crap—potato chips or pizza—and it was the only peace I could find. And it was always junk food. And then when I was in high school, I flew the other way and I barely ate."

She began to starve herself in an attempt to keep away the pain and the shame of not being good enough.

"I had a healthy weight as a child, but as a teenager I was very thin. I did not eat breakfast. I did not eat lunch. If I had lunch, it was a salad with no dressing, and then I would binge at night when I got home. When I was restricting my eating, I would obsess about my appearance and my size. I got into the game of comparison. I went to a very competitive high school where there was a high level of social pressure, and I immediately engaged in that comparison. I was never thin enough. I was athletic and I ran and was very active, but I felt just enormous."

When she went away to college, *"I did okay and maintained my weight pretty well. I think getting away from my mom did me a world of good."* But she was not able to escape from the part of herself that felt the shame of not being good enough.

"When I began building a career, my compulsive eating started almost immediately. I never felt intelligent because I didn't study hard in college or even in high school. I felt dull. And all of my friends got such great grades and I got by with passing grades. I really questioned my intelligence. And then I had to go out into this big work-world with a 3.0 GPA that I was so ashamed of. This, I thought, was my great shame and I felt inferior from the word 'go.' I started eating compulsively then and it just escalated. To cope with my feelings of inadequacy, I became obsessed with food.

"After I worked for a year or so, I decided to go to graduate school. I picked the top communications school in the county, determined to be perfect, to make up for past errors, and that's when the compulsive eating really kicked in.

"I was so scared and so shy inside, but I realized if I put my exterior together and looked a certain way, that got me so far. I gave people the impression that I was confident, really on the ball. And I started to rely on my exterior appearance. I became absolutely professional at looking fine, more than fine, looking like I was a stellar

achiever. And that's when my insides and my outsides started not to match. I became really obsessed with food to block out my inner feelings of shyness and insecurity that didn't match my confident exterior."

The more she tried to present only one side of herself to the outside world, the more difficult it became to keep her shadow side, her disowned feelings of inferiority, of shame and pain, confined to the underworld. Unwilling to remain hidden from view, her shadow sister was gaining strength and threatening to take over her life. In a frantic attempt to keep her away, *"I would make secret runs to the grocery store, secret runs to McDonald's. I remember one time late at night, I was lying on the couch agonizing over a McDonald's caramel sundae with nuts. I didn't live in a real great area, but I got up and drove to this horrible part of town because it has the closest McDonald's and got french fries and a sundae. That's when the real crazy behavior started. I remember coming home and feeling so out of control, having no sense of how to stop it.*

"My food volume really increased. I had no concept of my hunger. I was totally lost in every sense of the word and yet, marching out there every day looking as though I had it all together. The stress I put myself through was tremendous, and that's when I finally tumbled into a counseling center at the university.

"That began my journey toward recovery even though at that point it wasn't about food. I began to see that my mother's alcoholism had hurt me deeply. My compulsive eating continued to hum along at that time while I began to deal with that litany of characteristics that are inherent in an adult child of an alcoholic: low self-esteem, feeling not good enough, a whole medley of things.

"I got out of graduate school and went back into this profession. Now I had this very expensive master's degree, and the guilt that came out of that was incredible. I became determined to earn my value, my sense of self-worth, through this career. Through all this, my eating got worse and worse, and the bingeing became a constant thing. I was

drinking and smoking cigarettes. Even more than the alcohol, food was
what I couldn't control. I could control the alcohol.

"I got more therapy after graduate school, mostly to cope with the
frustrations of work and to help me come to terms with getting mar-
ried to my husband and the strong opposition from my parents. It was
yet another example of how inappropriate and controlling their behav-
ior was. They tried to influence me. They never valued that I loved
this person and wanted to spend the rest of my life with him. Oh,
God, no, that had no value at all."

Her journey was a long one. But she persisted, winding
around the periphery of the labyrinth, looking for the gateway that
would lead her toward freedom from her food and fat obsessions.
She found it by speaking her truth, by sharing her pain and shame
about her eating.

"At that time, I told my husband I don't want to have any secrets
in this marriage. I told him I have a terrible problem with eating. And
from then on I was very up front with him. I would hide from him
what I was eating but I would usually tell him later. He was wonder-
ful about it. It hurt him to see me destroying myself and he was so con-
cerned he wanted to help in any way, but he let it be my problem. He
didn't try to fix me, which I thank him so much for because I needed
to face this on my own and have his support for as long as I needed it,
but I couldn't have coped with him getting all involved."

She began with a weight loss program, in hot pursuit of her
runaway eating behavior. And like the Japanese woman who
chased after her runaway rice cakes, she found herself heading
toward a den where the Oni lived.

"After a while, I was able to lose forty pounds by cutting out a
lot of things and eating very healthy meals and exercising. But I knew
that the demon was still there, that I hadn't cured anything. By that
time, I knew that although I wasn't such an awful person, something
was wounded deep down inside of me. But I didn't know what it was.

And I knew that until I got to it, this would never go away. I used to pray to God that I would get to it."

She was able to maintain her weight for about seven months while she looked for a job. *"And literally the day I started in my new job, I started to gain weight."*

She began therapy again and joined a women's disordered eating group. This led her down the shadowy pathway toward where her demons lived. Along the way, she discovered the connection between her compulsive eating and her career.

"Because my mom was such a nightmare, I turned to my dad very early on and valued what he valued. I realized that I was trying to be more like his son than his daughter, to be his little 'protege.' My dad was very successful, and I wanted so desperately to win his approval so I could be like him, not like her. That's why I took the college route and the graduate school route to be a professional woman. He used to talk to me all the time about what kind of jobs he saw me in. They were all very glamorous professional positions. That's what he wanted for me. Having a family and not having a career was just heresy to my father. It wasn't something he valued. His ambition came from a loving place, but I think it was really misguided. And he liked it when I looked a certain way, when I had my coiffed hair and got my master's degree. Boy, I got big points with him for that. So I realized that all my efforts were to win his love and to align with him completely. Because that was the only safe place there was. That was survival."

When she arrived at that still point in the center of her being, she came face to face with her fears of inadequacy, the pain of never being good enough, of having no value, and the shame of her suffering.

"In therapy, I would tell my worst truths and learn to see that my disordered eating either had a reason or had value, that there was value in what I thought was so horrible. I began to see my eating as having a purpose, that it wasn't about 'I'm so diseased and broken.' Everybody had always been so quick to say, 'Too bad that you're like

this. How can we get you out of this? Let's fix you and get you better. I was always someone who needed to be fixed. Suddenly it was, 'Let's look at what that's about' as opposed to fixing it.

"And I finally got at what that poor, hurt place was and discovered that I was totally shamed as a child and made to feel as though I had no value except for maybe how I looked. I was so utterly and deeply shamed, and told that my value came from the exterior, how closely I could fit the standards of others. My insights, my ability to see the invisible, my sensitivity, were not valued in any way within my family."

She discovered the deep, dark shame and loathing she felt toward her disowned feminine self that her shadow sister had relentlessly tried to bring to her attention.

"Learning in therapy about the imbalance between the male and female energies within me was so important. I realize now that ever since I was a little girl, I absolutely abhorred women's things. I wanted a boy's bike, I wanted boy's tennis shoes. I didn't want to be a boy, but I wanted to be a woman that was so bold I could enter the man's world and have it work for me. I realize that is what has been fueling this career obsession and why I've been so reluctant to have a family.

"Until I got to know my inner feminine self, I had no understanding of my own pace and my own needs. That was totally alien to me. Every day there were things I had to do, a schedule I had to adjust to. I had to be up to what the day had in store for me, and if I wasn't up to it, I just beat myself. I realize now that I was totally out of synch with my feminine side, my rhythms, my intuition. Everything was shut off. No wonder I was so lost and so hungry. And so desperate. I see that so clearly now."

As she began to understand and embrace her feminine nature, she began to value and appreciate her dream world as a vast treasure-house of inner wisdom.

"It all came to light through my dreams. I learned to look at my dreams and use them, especially for learning about my inner mascu-

line and feminine selves. Working with my dreams was so important. I discovered over and over that dreams were an incredible source of information for me. Now I look forward to having them.

"I had always been so angry at myself because I found it so hard to get out of bed in the morning. I still do. But now I recognize that those dozing minutes are times of great insight. That is when my spirit, my soul, presents itself. Now I'm so grateful that I'm like that. And I just love to lie there in that half-and-half place. It's been really valuable."

And she began to appreciate the wisdom of her female body.

"When I stopped having my period, I saw it was all about this, to help me see how out of balance I was with my masculine and feminine sides. One of the most important pieces in this journey was learning to value my menstrual cycle and recognize how it gives me information. It draws out my intuititve side, which is so strong and so fully formed, and yet I had never paid attention to it. I learned to trust it and rejoice in the fact that I have a menstrual cycle. My period going away, that was the best thing that ever happened because it led me down this path."

Unable to reconcile with her own mother who remained alcoholic, she was nevertheless able to develop a strong inner mother who could nourish her and guide her toward acceptance and understanding of her feelings.

"I learned that when I feel the urge to binge, I'm not tuned in to what's happening in my life. I have not allowed myself to feel a feeling. And it's taken a long time to understand that feelings aren't right or wrong. That they are here to guide me. And if I have one and I ignore it, it's only going to get worse.

"It's all a part of the concept of eating when I'm hungry. And when I'm hungry, I don't want junk food. I say, 'Do you want cake or candy?' and I get 'No, I want a balanced diet.' Those food obsessions kick in when I'm not hungry, and then I know there's an emotional hunger I'm trying to feed with food. What's so funny is that I'm

starting to cook more. You would think that somebody obsessed with food would have cooked all the time. I never cooked. Now I'm taking the time to make nice dinners."

Having found the lost, rejected parts of herself, she was able to make her way out of the labyrinth.

"I see that I've been on an incredible journey. I like myself now. I value myself. Once I stopped relying on a fake exterior, the master's degree, and all the trappings of the career, I became open to wherever my life takes me.

"I find that I'm assertive, I'm strong, I'm brave, and I'm bright. All those things I kept trying to pretend to the world I was, I realized were within me all the time. That's so ironic to me.

"I feel more like the little girl I was at seven than that maniac I was at sixteen, or the scared Bambi I was at twenty-six. They are all in me but I feel much more like that little girl who walked down with her hair flying, who believed in herself and went about her life without having to have radar going to keep from being hurt. I've come back to that.

"For the first time in all of the work that I've done, I know that this time my recovery is real, genuine, because I got at what was so wounded inside of me. I can tune in, listen, and self-regulate. I have a sense of wholeness, a sense of self-worth. I know in my heart of hearts that I'm finally there."

And so you have it. Some of the stories of women who entered the labyrinth of recovery. Each woman's healing journey was one that took her not out into the world to seek her fortune, but, rather, into the dark center of her being.

She began this inward journey from a place of great pain and confusion in search of a reprieve from an obsession that persecuted her. Traveling at her own pace, with her daily feelings as her trusty companions, she made her way down this circular, twisting, winding path. She learned to rely on her bodily sensations, instincts, and natural rhythms; sometimes plodding, sometimes racing, sometimes waiting, sometimes resting. Along the way, she gained new skills and reclaimed old strengths as she discovered parts of herself that had been disowned and devalued. She encountered hungry ogres and voracious dragons that needed to be fed, not slain, so she could continue her journey.

To lighten her load on this sometimes long and difficult journey, she needed to discard old perceptions of herself and ways of relating to others. She had to find the courage to let go of old habits with food that had once upon a time been helpful.

Upon reaching the center of her being, she met up with the loving, nourishing Wise woman who lives within, whose sweet, strong voice would speak to her and teach her to fulfill her heart's desires.

And as she made her way back out into the world, guided by the soft, reflective light of the moon, she found herself getting stronger and stronger. Her step became lighter and easier, and she became more and more comfortable in her own skin. She had the courage to speak her truth, over and over, and the strength to set her limits, time and time again, so others could not trample on her newfound self.

And so it was she found her way home.

Resources

EDAP (Eating Disorders Awareness and Prevention)
603 Stewart St., Suite 803, Seattle, WA 98101 (206) 382-3587
Hotline: 1-800-931-2237
www.edap.org
   National organization dedicated to increasing the awareness and prevention of eating disorders through distribution of educational materials, prevention programs, newsletter, and conferences. Sponsors Eating Disorders Awareness Week in February with a network of state coordinators.

Gürze Books
P.O. Box 2238, Carlsbad, CA 92018   1-800-756-7533
www.bulimia.com
   Free eating disorders resource catalogue. Comprehensive selection of self-help books, professional texts, and educational videos.

Health Wisdom for Women
Christiane Northrup, M.D.
12 Portland St., Yarmouth, ME 04096 1-800-804-0935
   Monthly newsletter that updates women's health information and resources. Emphasizes the impact of thoughts, emotions, and behaviors on physical health. Audio and video tapes available through website.

Isabella
2780 Via Orange Way, Suite B, Spring Valley, CA 91978
1-800-777-5205
   Free catalogue of books and tools to help reclaim the Feminine and bring balance to families, political systems, businesses, spirituality, and health care.

Ladyslipper
Music by Women
P.O. Box 3124-R, Durham, NC 27715 1-800-634-6044
Listen Line: (919) 644-0000
www.ladyslipper.org
Comprehensive catalog devoted to the musical accomplishments of women artists and musicians. Listen line allows callers to hear samples of music.

Monte Nido
27162 Sea Vista Drive, Malibu, CA 90265 (310) 457-9958
www.montenido.com
Residential treatment facility designed and created by recovered professionals to heal women suffering from anorexia, bulimia, and exercise addiction. Promotes the idea that eating disordered individuals can be fully recovered where issues of food, exercise, and body image are no longer necessary as a means of self-expression and are not used in destructive ways.

The Renfrew Center
475 Spring Lane, Philadelphia, PA 19128 1-800-RENFREW
www.renfrew.org
Residential treatment facilities in Pennsylvania and Florida. Outpatient treatment services provided in New York and New Jersey. Program designed exclusively to help women resolve eating disorders and women's mental health issues. Treatment philosophy is built on a model of empowerment, respect, and collaboration.

Rosewood
36075 South Rincon Rd., Wickenburg, AZ 85390 1-800-280-1212
www.eatingdisorder.net
Women's center for anorexia, bulimia, and related disorders. Residential facility that emphasizes empowerment, dignity, and honor for women and their life events.

Suggested Reading

Bolen, Jean Shinoda. *Goddesses in Everywoman: A New Psychology of Women*. San Francisco, CA: HarperCollins, 1984.

Butler, Pamela E. *Self-Assertion For Women*. New York: HarperCollins, 1992.

Chernin, Kim. *The Obsession: Reflections on the Tyranny of Slenderness*. New York: HarperCollins, 1981.

_____. *The Hungry Self: Women, Eating & Identity*. New York: HarperCollins, 1985.

Costin, Caroline. *The Eating Disorder Sourcebook: A Comprehensive Guide to the Causes, Treatment, and Prevention of Eating Disorders*. Lincolnwood, IL: NTC Publishing, 1996.

Duerk, Judith. *Circle of Stones: Woman's Journey to Herself*. San Diego, CA: LuraMedia, 1989.

_____. *I Sit Listening to the Wind: Woman's Encounter Within Herself*. San Diego, CA: LuraMedia, 1993.

Eisler, Riane. *The Chalice and the Blade*. San Francisco, CA: HarperCollins, 1987.

Estes, Clarissa Pinkola. *Women Who Run With the Wolves: Myths and Stories of the Wild Woman Archetype*. New York: Ballantine Books, 1992.

Gawain, Shakti. *Living in the Light: A Guide to Personal and Planetary Transformation*. San Rafael, CA: New World Library, 1986.

Gimbutas, Maria. *Goddesses and Gods of Old Europe, 7000-3500 B.C.* Berkeley: University of CA Press, 1982.

Gray, John. *Mars and Venus in the Bedroom: A Guide to Lasting Romance and Passion.* New York: HarperCollins, 1995.

Harper, Linda R. *The Tao of Eating: Feeding Your Soul Through Everyday Experiences with Food.* Philadelphia, PA: Innisfree Press, 1998.

Lerner, Harriet. *The Dance of Anger: A Woman's Guide to Changing Patterns of Intimate Relationships.* New York: HarperCollins, 1985

Northrup, Christiane. *Women's Bodies, Women's Wisdom: Creating Physical and Emotional Health and Healing.* New York: Bantam Books, 1994.

Mann, Judy. *The Difference: Growing Up Female In America.* New York: Warner Books, 1994.

Orbach, Susie. *Fat is a Feminist Issue: the Anti-Diet Guide to Permanent Weight Loss.* New York: Berkley Books, 1982.

Orenstein, Peggy. *SchoolGirls: Young Women Self-Esteem, and the Confidence Gap.* New York: Doubleday, 1994.

Owen, Laura. *Her Blood is Gold: Celebrating the Power of Menstruation.* New York: HarperCollins, 1993.

Radcliff, Rebecca Ruggles. *Body Prayers: Finding Body Peace.* Minneapolis, MN: EASE, 1999

_____. *Enlightened Eating: Understanding and Changing Your Relationship with Food.* Minneapolis, MN: EASE, 1996.

_____. *Dance Naked in Your Living Room: Handling Stress & Finding Joy*. Minneapolis, MN: EASE, 1997.

Roth, Geneen. *Feeding the Hungry Heart: the Experience of Compulsive Eating*. New York: Penguin Putnam, Inc, 1982.

_____. *Breaking Free From Compulsive Eating*. New York: Penguin Putnam, Inc., 1984.

_____. *When Food is Love: Exploring the Relationship Between Eating and Intimacy*. New York: Putnam, Inc., 1991.

_____. *Why Weight? A Guide to Ending Compulsive Eating*. New York: Penguin Putnam, Inc., 1989.

Schwartz, Bob. *Diets Don't Work: the Secrets of Losing Weight Step-By-Step When All Else Fails*. Houston, Texas: Breakthru, 1982.

_____. *Diets Still Don't Work: How to Lose Weight Step-By-Step Even After You've Failed at Dieting*. Houston, Texas: Breakthru, 1990.

Shuttle, Penelope and Redgrove, Peter. *The Wise Wound: Myths, Realities, and Meanings of Menstruation*. New York: Bantam Books, 1990.

Sjoo, Monica and Mor, Barbara. *The Great Cosmic Mother: Rediscovering the Religion of the Earth*. New York: HarperCollins, 1987.

Signal, Karen A. *Wisdom of the Heart: Working with Women's Dreams*. New York: Bantam Books, 1990.

Stone, Merlin. *When God Was A Woman*. New York: Harcourt Brace Jovanovich, 1976.

Sward, Sharon Norfleet. *You Are More Than What You Weigh: Improve Your Self-Esteem No Matter What Your Weight.* Denver, CO: Wholesome Publishers, 1998.

Vanzant, Iyanla. *Yesterday I Cried: Celebrating the Lessons of Living and Loving.* New York: Simon & Schuster, 1998.

Walker, Barbara. *Feminist Fairy Tales.* San Francisco, CA: HarperCollins, 1996.

Williamson, Marianne. *A Woman's Worth.* New York: Ballantine Books, 1993.

Wolf, Naomi. *The Beauty Myth: How Images of Beauty Are Used Against Women.* New York: HarperCollins, 1991.

Woodman, Marion. *Conscious Femininity.* Toronto, Canada: Inner City Books, 1993.

$\mathcal{M}$ost of the tales in this book are traditional folktales and myths that have been told and retold by generations of women. Earlier versions of the stories retold in this book can be found in the following books: "The Buried Moon," in *More English Fairy Tales* (1904), Joseph Jacobs. "The Emperor's New Clothes" and "The Ugly Duckling," in *The Complete Andersen: All of the 168 Stories* (1949), Hans Christian Andersen, translated by Jean Hersholt. "The Name of the Tree," in *The Name of the Tree* (1989), Celia Barker Lottridge. "The Stars in the Sky," in *More English Fairy Tales* (1904), Joseph Jacobs, and in *The Maid of the North* (1981), Ethel Johnston Phelps. "The Old Woman and the Rice Cakes," in *Tales of Laughter* (1908), Kate D. Wiggins, and in *The Maid of the North* (1981), Ethel Johnston Phelps. "The Tutu Bird," in *Old World and New World Fairy Tales* (1966), Anabel Williams-Ellis. "Elsa and the Evil Wizard," in *Old Swedish Fairy Tales* (1925), Anna Wahlenberg, translated by A. DeC. Patterson, and in *The Maid of the North* (1981), Ethel Johnston Phelps. "The Princess and the Goddess," in *Sage Woman Magazine* (Spring 1989), Lunaea Weatherstone. "The Lute Player," in *The Violet Fairy Book* (1901), Andrew Lang, and in *Tatterhood and Other Tales* (1978), Ethel Johnston Phelps. "The Wonderful Pearl," in *The Woman in the Moon* (1985), James Riordan. "Sirena," in *The Guam Recorder* (October 1933), Lagrimas P. Leon Guerrero. "The Peddler's Dream," in *British Folk Tales* (1977), Katherine Briggs. "The Magic Pear Tree," in *Chinese Fairytales and Fantasies* (1979), Moss Roberts. "What a Woman Desires Most" is an old tale that can be found in Chaucer's *Canterbury Tales*, published in the late 1300's and in *The Story of King Arthur and His Knights* (1903), Howard Pyle. "The Tiger's Whisker," in *The Tiger's Whisker* (1959), Harold Courlander. "Inanna's Descent," in *Descent to the Goddess* (1981), Sylvia Brinton Perera.

About the Author

ables, folk tales, and legends have always played a crucial role in the life and work of psychologist Anita Johnston. As a child growing up in a multicultural extended family on the island of Guam, she was nurtured by strong women who taught important values and lessons about life through the stories they told and the songs they sang. Her mother, an American who married a Chamorro man, was a librarian whose personal collection was filled with legends of ancient peoples, accounts of early Spanish explorers, and heroic tales from World War II, including those about her paternal grandmother who led the underground resistance movement during the Japanese occupation of Guam. It was also the traditional tales, told by the Chamorro and Filipina women who cared for Dr. Johnston and her six siblings, that gave her a sense of the power of stories to enlighten and instill change.

Her interest in female psychology and the role of women in contemporary society sprang from her experience as a contestant in the Miss Universe contest when she was 18 years old. Her observations of what society dictated as feminine beauty, as opposed to the lessons learned from the women in her family, were a driving force in her decision to become a psychologist. After getting her B.S. and M.A. in psychology, she received her Ph.D. in clinical psychology in 1980.

In response to the increasing numbers of women with disordered eating, Dr. Johnston cofounded the Anorexia and Bulimia Center of Hawaii in 1982. In addition to her private practice, she lectures widely to professional organizations, universities, medical institutions and the community at large. She lives with her husband and two daughters in Hawaii.

About the Publisher

Since 1980, Gürze Books has specialized in quality information on eating disorders recovery, research, education, advocacy, and prevention. Gürze publishes books in this field, as well as the *Eating Disorders Review,* a clinical newsletter for professionals. They also distribute *The Eating Disorders Resource Catalogue,* which is used as a resource throughout the world. Their website (www.gurze.com) is an excellent Internet gateway to treatment facilities, associations, basic facts, and other eating disorders sites.

ORDER FORM

Eating in the Light of the Moon is available at bookstores and libraries or may be ordered directly from Gürze Books.

The Eating Disorders Resource Catalogue has more than 125 books on eating disorders and related topics, including body image, size-acceptance, self-esteem, and more. It is a valuable resource that also includes basic facts about eating disorders, and listings of non-profit associations and treatment facilities. It is handed out by therapists, educators, and other health care professionals throughout the world.

___ FREE copies of the *Eating Disorders Resource Catalogue*.

___ copies of *Eating in the Light of the Moon*.
$13.95 plus $2.90 each for shipping.

Quantity discounts are available.

NAME_____

ADDRESS_____

CITY, ST, ZIP _____

PHONE_____

Gürze Books (EIL)
P.O. Box 2238
Carlsbad, CA 92018
(800) 757-7533 fax (760)434-5476
www.gurze.com